JUST LIKE THE COUNTRY

MEMORIES OF LONDON FAMILIES
THE NEW COTTAGE ESTATES 1919-1939

Edited By Antonia Rubinstein
with Andy Andrews and Pam Schweitzer

Photography by Alex Schweitzer

Research by Antonia Rubinstein, Pauline Devaney, Pamela Lyne,
Andy Andrews and Pam Schweitzer

Foreword by Rod Hackney
Past President of The Royal Institute of British Architects

'Just Like The Country' is published by Age Exchange to coincide with their
theatre production of a musical play with the same title.

Model of two blocks of cottages to be erected at Roehampton

AGE EXCHANGE GRATEFULLY ACKNOWLEDGES GENEROUS FINANCIAL SUPPORT FOR THIS
PROJECT FROM THE DORON FOUNDATION, THE LONDON BOROUGHS GRANTS SCHEME,
THE FORD MOTOR COMPANY AND MARKS AND SPENCER.

CONTRIBUTORS

Florrie Abel
Leslie Charles Alder
Edwin Hardy Amies
Arthur Andrews
Vera Andrews
Lilian Badger
Dorothy Barton
Lilian Beardsmore
Tina Belton
Donald Breeze
Stanley Breeze
Mr Brooke
Violet Bunyon
Ron Chattington

Amelia Cogley
Bob Cubitt
Len Dunning
Harvey Edmonds
Florence Essam
George Evans
Rosina Evans
Jim Evans
Amy Ewell
Alfred Gates
Hetty Gates
Bill Hahn
Gladys Hanson
George Herbert

Mr Hibbert
Mrs Hibbert
Peggy Iris
Alice Ivison
Beatrice Kitchen
Elizabeth Knight
Sir Maurice Laing
Betty Mapstone
Mrs Martin
Daphne Maynard
Joyce Milan
May Millbank
Eric Phillips
Doris Pinion

Annie Prendergast
Phyllis Rhoden
Marjorie Rutty
John Edwin Smith
Mr Spicer
Irene Swanton
Mrs Tanner
Ted Knightley
Bill Waghorn
Martha Wall
Bert Wallis
Mabel Wallis
Ken Wills
Ivy Woollett

Arthur, Richard and Toby from Downham, Vi from St Helier and Patricia and Winifred from Bellingham.

St Helier Estate

With grateful thanks to the following organisations and individuals for their help:

Mr Rice of The Rendezvous Club, Becontree; Sue Curtis and Sue Kelly from Valence House Library, Becontree; Joan Spendlove from Brocklebank Lodge, Becontree; The Dagenham Girl Pipers; Del Pasterfield and David Wise of The Ford Motor Company; Vera Andrews and the Downham Reminiscence Group; Mel Wright of Lewisham Social Services; Carl Harrison of Manor House Local History Library; St Helier Senior Citizens' Club; Gabriel Genest and Roehampton Luncheon Club; Peter Willmott; Mr Petty of Roehampton Tenants' Association; Richmond Upon Thames Council Housing Department; The Royal Institute of British Architects; Mike Evans and Chris Denver of the Greater London Record Office and Library; Ann Fletcher of the London Transport Museum.

Photographs and documents kindly loaned by the Greater London Photographic Library, Valence House Library and the contributors.

Picture Credits: Greater London Photographic Library: pages 1, 2, 3, 8, 9, 10, 11, 12, 14, 15, 17, 18, 19, 21, 24, 26, 28, 29, 35, 37, 38, 39, 42, 43, 46, 49, 51, 54, 55, 61, 69, 70, 72, 73, 75, 81, 83, 87, 91. Valence House Library: pages 4, 5, 7, 13, 30, 31, 32, 33, 34, 36, 47, 48, 54, 56, 59, 60, 67, 71, 74, 77, 80, 84, 90, 91.

Transcription by Antonia Rubinstein, Barnaby Brown, John Shergold, Andy Andrews and Pamela Lyne.

CONTENTS

The Pleasance, Roehampton, looking north, Sept 1924

Variety of house fronts, Becontree

HOMES FOR THE PEOPLE

'THE BUILDER'. 8 NOVEMBER 1918

If the hundreds of thousands of cottages for the working classes, which it is expected will be built with Governmental assistance, are to become real homes in which men and women are to spend contented lives, and bring up happy children, sound in mind and body, then the task is one worthy of the best and most sympathetic consideration of everyone concerned. To bring about such a beneficial result will demand a keen and high degree of intelligence not only from statesmen, but also from men and women of affairs and practical experience.

By rights, many of the requisite houses should be built before demobilization takes place. It is known that in certain areas, because of the cessation of building operations during the war, and by the deterioration of accommodation which has inevitably taken place, overcrowding in dwellings otherwise suitable has resulted, and that dwellings continue to be occupied which in normal circumstances could no longer be regarded as suitable at all. Pressure, in short, has produced and intensified slums, and it is in these slums that the families of many of our brave soldiers now live, and to which they will have to return, unless a great effort is made to deal immediately with a substantial part of a housing programme. Instead of

looking at this proposition as a pauperising one, as is the tendency in certain quarters, should we not consider the State contribution as a free gift to the success of a scheme intended in some extent to signify our indebtedness to the five million soldiers and three million munition workers who have so bravely done their part in keeping these shores free from the arrogance and ruthlessness of an unscrupulous enemy?

We should see to it that for all time the families of old soldiers and sailors have the first right to the occupation of the model houses which it is the nation's purpose to erect and let at modest and, no doubt, uneconomic rents.

But before any building is done, it is necessary to know first, exactly what sort of houses are required in the different localities; and, secondly, where exactly these houses should be placed. Cottages can not be designed on paper; cottages are the result of practical experience. At one time it was thought anyone could design a house, but now we are beginning to understand that if these dwellings are to become real homes, convenient habitations for successive families for many years to come, then each is worthy of the highest consideration.

FOREWORD

BY ROD HACKNEY

'Just Like The Country' provides a fascinating view of one of the most significant periods of change in the history of mass housing provision in the years following the First World War, and the Government's promise to provide 'homes fit for heroes'.

The suspension of the building programme during the Great War meant that conditions in London's inner city slums could scarcely have been worse. This situation is vividly documented here in descriptions of extreme overcrowding, severe lack of basic amenities and the foul environment, all problems caused and compounded by the poverty which was so widespread in the recession years of the twenties and early thirties.

Although the sense of community is strongly conveyed in these descriptions too, nevertheless simple considerations of health and welfare necessitated the movement of thousands of people out of the inner cities. In spite of fears at the prospect, they left their communities of friends and relations for places that many had never seen, at a time when the sites of most of the new LCC estates were, for all practical purposes, out of reach in the country.

Striking examples of the painful process of creating a new community, in circumstances which sometimes included a lack of infrastructure as well as medical or educational facilities, show just how strong was the 'feeling of the times' on the LCC estates in overcoming the initial problems, not only as a result of sharing backgrounds and burdens, and particularly that of poverty, but also due to a desire to share opportunity and progress.

The scale and urgency of the demand for development between the two World Wars have a number of parallels with the extensive re-development undertaken during the latter half of the 1980s and continuing into the 1990s. There is a lesson for today's developers and architects, in terms of the requirement for accurate and sympathetic assessment of the needs of tenants, in those instances described here where the fears of those uprooted from close-knit communities in the inner cities were matched by poor planning or design on the LCC estates. Moreover today, with

the advantage of a further sixty years' experience, there is much more scope for environmentally appropriate and imaginative response on the part of the designer.

For all the startling medical, technical and sociological advances since the 1930s which can now meet the majority of the needs which were most pressing at the beginning of the century, there are too many people still living in poor conditions for this to be read simply as an engaging history. Equally, at a time when a combination of factors – immeasurably improved transport, the decline in the traditional industries and subsequently shifting labour markets – has eroded first the self-sufficiency and then the stability of so many long-established centres of population, we are perhaps in greater danger than ever of neglecting the value of the community.

'Just Like The Country' is an absorbing glimpse of the past as well as an apt reminder of the potential strength and vitality of the community, and the tributes paid by many of the LCC tenants of the twenties and thirties to their Cottage Estates are a timely testimony to the best that state-provided rented housing can be.

An excellent example of adaptation of natural surroundings. Becontree, 1926

INTRODUCTION

BY ANTONIA RUBINSTEIN

'Just Like The Country' presents the reminiscences of Londoners who moved from the inner-city slum dwellings to the spacious 'cottage estates', built by the London County Council between 1919 and 1939.

Of the thirteen London estates built during this period, we at Age Exchange have collected memories relating to eight of them: Becontree, Bellingham, Castelnau, Downham, Mottingham, Roehampton, St Helier and Watling.

During the last three years, we have interviewed many pensioners from all over London who were rehoused on these 'cottage estates' in the inter-war years. We were also able to find people who were either involved in the building of the estates or worked for the LCC, and their recollections provide a unique record of the working conditions and methods of the period.

Before 1914, living conditions for many in central London were atrocious. A chronic shortage of housing meant that thousands of people lived in overcrowded and unhealthy accommodation. It took the First World War to reveal that Britain was a 'C3' nation with many of the men who volunteered for the forces being turned away due to ill health. The problem of inadequate housing and its relationship with poor health could no longer be ignored and, after the war, it became obvious to those in power that measures had be to be taken. A better start in life was also required for the younger generation.

Housing became a major political issue, with Lloyd George advocating, in his election campaign, that Great Britain should be a 'land fit for heroes to live in'. The Housing Act of 1919 was the direct result of these election promises. This made all local authorities responsible for the supply of houses for the less well-off in need of accommodation. The LCC was quick to respond to the new legislation and undertook the construction of a number of 'cottage estates' on the outskirts of London. The houses were built to improved standards in design and comfort. Not only were they light and spacious, they also included an indoor lavatory and bathroom. Each house was set in its own garden, so that children could exercise outside in an enclosed safe space while also benefitting from the cleaner atmosphere.

LONDON COUNTY COUNCIL

HOUSING ESTATES, Etc.

Particulars are given below of each of the Council's Housing Estates, arranged alphabetically under the headings (1) Cottage Estates, (2) Block Dwellings, etc., and (3) Lodging Houses. The Index numbers correspond with those shown enclosed in circles on the face of the map.

COTTAGE ESTATES

1	BECONTREE, Essex.—2,770 acres. 25,769 houses and flats completed. 1 to 6 rooms. 56 houses to be erected.
2	BELLINGHAM, Lewisham.—252 acres. 2,676 houses and flats. 1 to 5 rooms. Completed.
3	CASTELNAU, Barnes.—51 acres. 644 houses. 3 to 5 rooms. Completed.
4	CHINGFORD, Essex.—187 acres. 168 houses and flats completed. 1 to 5 rooms. 249 houses and flats in course of erection. A further 1,151 houses and flats proposed to be erected.
5	DOWNHAM, Lewisham and Bromley.—600 acres. 7,097 houses and flats completed. 1 to 5 rooms. A further 14 houses and flats proposed to be erected.
6	GRANGE HILL SITE, Essex.—434 acres. Proposals under consideration.
7	HANWELL, Ealing.—140 acres. 1,586 houses and flats. 1 to 5 rooms. Completed.
8	HEADSTONE LANE, Harrow.—142 acres. Development under consideration.
9	KENMORE PARK, Middlesex.—58 acres. 652 houses and flats. 1 to 5 rooms. Completed.
10	KIDBROOKE, Greenwich.—68 acres. About 834 houses and flats proposed to be erected.
11	MOTTINGHAM, Bromley, Lewisham, Chislehurst and Sidcup.—202 acres. 2,337 houses and flats. 1 to 5 rooms. Completed.
12	NORBURY, Croydon.—28 acres. 717 houses. 3 to 5 rooms. Completed.
13	OLD OAK, Hammersmith and Acton.—46 acres. 1,056 houses and flats. 1 to 5 rooms. Completed.
14	ROEHAMPTON, Wandsworth.—147 acres. 1,212 houses and flats. 2 to 5 rooms. Completed.
15	ST. HELIER, Surrey.—825 acres. 9,075 houses and flats. 1 to 5 rooms. Completed.
16	THORNHILL, Greenwich.—20½ acres. 380 houses and flats. 1 to 5 rooms. Completed.
17	TOTTERDOWN FIELDS, Wandsworth.—39 acres. 1,262 houses and flats. 2 to 5 rooms. Completed.
18	WATLING, Middlesex.—386 acres. 4,034 houses and flats. 2 to 5 rooms. Completed.
19	WHITE HART LANE, Tottenham and Wood Green.—138 acres. 2,230 houses and flats. 2 to 5 rooms. Completed.
20	WORMHOLT, Hammersmith.—68 acres. 895 houses and flats. 2 to 5 rooms. Completed.

BLOCK DWELLINGS, Etc.

26	ADA PLACE, Bethnal Green.—77 dwellings. 2 to 5 rooms. Completed.
27	ALBANY ROAD, Camberwell.—28 dwellings in course of erection. 2 to 4 rooms. A further 132 dwellings proposed to be erected.
28	ALBERTA HOUSE, Poplar.—39 dwellings. 2 to 4 rooms. Completed.

Making a move to a 'cottage estate' was, for many people, a momentous decision to take. The communities of inner London were formidably close-knit, and to leave them behind for a new life in the 'country' involved a degree of personal sacrifice. Times were insecure for much of the 1920s and the fear of unemployment meant that certain risks were inevitable. Renting a house on an estate yet to establish itself, often a long way from the work place, introduced new demands and responsibilities, which were to have serious implications for community growth and development.

Yet, 'Just Like The Country' demonstrates how bravely people confronted these challenges. Those who were parents gradually adapted to the new way of life, and after a period of time, the 'community feeling' began to establish itself. The accounts of people who were children at the time convey the great sense of excitement generated by attending new schools, meeting new friends, and exploring the environment around their home.

'Just Like The Country' is not intended to be an academic study of each estate. The book is a collection of reminiscences linked by a common theme. My role as editor and researcher was to encourage the contributors to record their experiences and generate discussion. I approached the research, not just through the text book, but by going into the communities and talking to the people who had helped to establish them.

We visited each estate and got in touch with local community centres, reminiscence groups, social and luncheon clubs. We met with people in their own homes, and it was very exciting to find some of the contributors still living in the houses originally allocated to them. The people we talked to always made us feel most welcome, and they were very generous in sharing their experiences.

All the stories used in 'Just Like The Country' have been taken from taped interviews. Our contributors were asked to explain why and how they applied to the LCC, and then to trace their progress, from the move itself, through the settling in period to the eventual creation of their new communities. They were asked to recall specific incidents, for example what they felt when they first saw their new house, or what it was like to have a garden or a proper bathroom for the first time in their lives.

I decided not to cover each estate individually because the experience of moving and those first impressions were, for most people, regardless of the estate, remarkably similar. Where the accounts differ is in how each family settled into the community and adapted to the new way of living. It was fascinating to see how quickly each estate evolved its own character, the location and size playing a large part in determining the way the community eventually developed.

All our contributors emphasised in their interviews how much the quality of their families' lives improved, and that being part of an estate community provided all kinds of new opportunities. I have therefore concluded 'Just Like The Country' with a very brief overview, summing up the enormous impact which these estates had upon the lives of those who moved to them.

I would like to thank all those people who helped to make 'Just Like The Country' possible: Pam Schweitzer for giving me the opportunity to carry out this fascinating study which I hope will inspire and interest the reader as much as it did me, Barnaby Brown for his accurate transcribing, and Andy Andrews for putting the final touches to the manuscript. Finally I would like to express my gratitude to the contributors themselves because, without their support, enthusiasm, and willingness to share their experiences, the project would not have been possible and their valuable memories would have gone unrecorded.

Alternate use of brick and white and coloured concrete, Becontree

HOMES FIT FOR HEROES

Foggy rooftops, Brady Street area, 1922

LIVING CONDITIONS BEFORE THE MOVE

My father died when I was three, so my mother moved us from above the coal shop in Walworth Road, South East London, to two rooms in Vauxhall Mansions, Lambeth.

Don't ask what life was like then in those two rooms. Mother used to take in washing. I can see her now, an orange box with a bath on top, rubbing the clothes clean and her legs bad with fibrositis from all the standing. There was a big mangle and Mother would give those that could a penny a time to turn the mangle and the clothes would then be dried around the fire.

On Saturdays, we had to lay in bed while Mother washed all our underclothes. I remember she'd hang the clothes round the fire, so we had all this steam in our room when we was asleep. On Sunday the underclothes would be all clean again. And that's how we went on.

We wasn't alright for food then. Mother always went without but we didn't. I remember the time we'd only have a cup of cocoa and a pound of broken biscuits for dinner. In those days you could go round to the soup shop, where you'd get a penny bowl of pea soup, but you had to take your own bread. On Friday when Mother got paid, we'd have pie and mash and that was a luxury.

Mother cooked on this big range, which was in the same room as half of us slept in, and I can remember the coal man come to shoot the coal in the coal box which was under the window. Because Mother couldn't afford anything else, I slept in an iron cot and that was my bed until I was fifteen.

Betty Mapstone (Becontree)

*Hatfield Street, Southwark, showing backstreet shops, rag and general merchant,
and fruiterer, 1923*

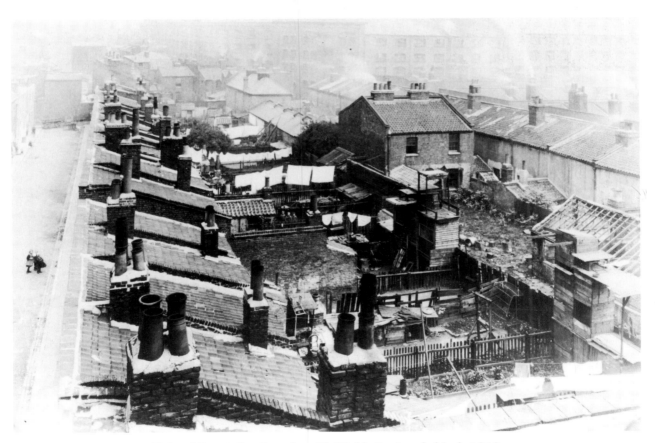

Tabard Street, Southwark, with Pink's Factory behind, 1918

BUGS IN THE BED

We lived in three upstairs rooms in Battersea, my parents and nine children. We had no garden so we used to run about in the streets. Mum and Dad had the front room and us lot shared the other ones. There were five to my bed, three up and two down. Our old house was buggy. They looked like black ladybirds, in every room they were flying everywhere. They didn't bite but crawled all over the place and we'd have to knock them out of the beds. They'd breed very quick. It was terrible!

Harvey Edmonds (Becontree)

Before my father died we lived in a bug-ridden house in Walworth. It was a private tenancy and we had two rooms, which we ate, slept and did everything in. Within two months of my father dying, the London County Council moved us out to some flats in Westminster.

We still only had two bedrooms there, so my sister and I slept with my mother and the boys all slept in the other room. I remember that first night in the flat, a cousin of mine said, "Aunty, do you know there are bugs in this room?". When my mother heard that she just wept.

I wonder how she managed then because she only had the widow's pension of ten shillings a week. That was her sole income and you didn't get money from the Poor Law, you just got food. My eldest brother and sister worked in London but they only earned seven-and-six. Mother always used to say, "Never mind, one day we will have a home. We will have a nice home."

She was a fighter and after the flat had been fumigated she was determined to get us out. Some old neighbours had moved to Middleton Road on the St Helier Estate so my mother went to see them. When she saw their place she said, "That's for us."

Vi (St Helier)

Mander Place, Union Street, Southwark, 1923

A COMPLAINING LANDLADY

We had a couple of rooms in Catford and our landlady wasn't very co-operative. She didn't like children and would complain about our child making a noise. I mean what noise does a child make when it's running around in bare feet? And I wasn't one to stand for that.

Hetty Gates (St Helier)

Tabard Garden area before clearance, 1913

Stepney, 1923

SOMEHOW WE MANAGED

We used to live in the top end of Tanners Hill, Deptford. The houses were very tiny and close together and it was just like a little village. We had two rooms in my uncle's and aunt's house. They had two daughters and at one time we had great aunt Harriet there as well. I don't know where we all slept but we managed. We had no running water at all in the house and every time you wanted to fill the kettle you had to go outside to the wash house, in the garden.

Of course we all lived close together but we knew everybody and everybody knew us. My father's mother, and his twelve brothers and sisters, lived in and around Deptford. My father used to take us round to see Grandma every Sunday morning. Some of the other relations would come too. She had a tiny sitting room and those that couldn't fit in would be sitting up the stairs. The children would be sent outside to play. We were one big happy family then and I loved Deptford.

Unfortunately I became sick and the doctor said I was to get out of Deptford so my parents got half a house in Fossdene Road, Charlton. We had two bedrooms, a living room and a small kitchen with a gas cooker and a range. There was no bathroom and we shared the toilet, which was downstairs, with the people who lived below us.

Dorothy Barton (St Helier)

22 Red Lion Street showing the range, 1929

ILL HEALTH

There were eight of us living in three rooms in Paddington, and we were overcrowded. We had to find new accommodation because of my father's health, he had TB (Tuberculosis).

Tina Belton (Roehampton)

We lived in the Peabody Buildings over Hammersmith Bridge and there were about sixty steps up to our flat. My brother had heart problems and couldn't do the stairs. The doctor gave my mother a letter to take to the council and that's how it went from there.

Mrs Tanner (Castelnau)

Mother had bronchitis and had been advised to move from North London to Downham because of the air, which at that time was considered to be good. My father didn't have a job at the time and it was years before he found work, so it was because of my mother that we got the house.

Vera Andrews (Downham)

Upper Ground Place, Southwark, 1923

11

THE TIN BATH

When Father came out of the Navy, after the First World War, he went straight to work in the Docks. Because he had regular work, we never knew poverty like some did, some had to run about with no shoes.

There were five of us living in this flat, overlooking the Thames. We had two rooms and a kind of kitchenette-cum-scullery affair with a sink. From our bedroom you could see all the tugs and boats going by. Between us and the river, we was facing the local tipping for the waste rubbish to go onto the Thames. The dust carts used to come along and they were all emptied into a shoot which went into a barge. Looking back on it, it couldn't have been very healthy, living where we did, what with all that dust and God knows what in the air.

We had no bathroom and every Friday night we had a bath in the tin bath. We would have to heat the water up by kettle. If you were the first one in, it was lovely but if you were the last! When we got too big to sit in the tin bath we were sent to the public baths.

These baths served about eight or nine blocks of flats and were in the middle of our buildings. Mother used to give us a towel and some soap and we'd go and take our turn in the bath queue. When we got inside we were given a bath cubicle with a number. I remember if our water was too hot we'd shout out, "Cold in number four," and they'd turn on the cold water for you.

Florence Essam (Becontree)

Brady Street Area, 1923

NO LOO!

I'd come from buildings in Whitechapel and we never had a lavatory. On each landing there would be four flats and a wash house. In the wash house was the lavatory, a ladies and a gents. Unfortunately they were filthy and rotten and absolutely vandalised. My father would never go there. We had buckets in our flat for the widdle, anything other than that, my father would do it on paper, because he just couldn't in the lavatory.

George Herbert (Becontree)

Old Castle Street, Aldgate. Slum tenements backing on to a school, 1919

ABSOLUTELY DISGUSTED

We lived in Paddington and by today's standards it was a pretty awful place though as a child I thought it had a great charm to it. The toilet was out in the backyard and we didn't have any water in our flat. You had to bring the water upstairs from the outhouse in jugs. If you wanted to wash, you would heat the water up on the stove. Then you put an oilcloth on a big table. You had your bowl on the table and you washed from there. When you had a bath, the tin bath would be brought out and you would bath in front of the fire like you see in the old films, with the miners. That's how it was in London.

My father was absolutely disgusted. He had gone through the war, been badly injured, and there were supposed to be homes fit for heroes but there weren't any. He put his name down on the housing list in 1919 and it took eight years for something to crop up.

Phyllis Rhoden (Downham)

BUILDING THE COTTAGE ESTATES

'THE WATLING RESIDENT'. MAY 1928

Owing to the high cost of postwar building, the erection of small houses to be let at weekly rentals ceased to be a remunerative proposition, with the result that this class of house lost its attraction to the speculative builder. Members of the working class were unable to pay remunerative rents and the burden of providing housing for them fell upon the shoulders of the local authorities and even they were unable to bear this burden without financial assistance from the government and a contribution from the rates.

In dealing with the complex problem of providing housing accommodation for the working classes, one of the initial difficulties is the selection of adequate and suitable sites at a reasonable price.

There are many points to be borne in mind when considering the suitability of a site required for a housing estate, such as accessibility, its capability for economic development, facilities for drainage, lighting, water supplies, travelling facilities, cheap fares, proximity to factories etc. These are important matters which must be carefully and seriously considered before any definite decision can be made regarding the acquisition of a site.

A compact estate of nearly 390 acres has been secured named 'Watling Estate' after the famous thoroughfare of that name constructed by the Romans. The land is undulating in character and well wooded. The Silk Stream runs through part of the estate. These natural conditions afford the opportunity of carrying out an attractive development of the property and limits the number of houses to be erected to a rate of twelve per acre.

A total of forty-one acres has been allocated for open spaces. Sites have also been provided for Churches. The Local Education Authority is acquiring five sites for the erection of elementary schools, and building operations on some of these have commenced. A large site on the north-eastern corner is being reserved for a secondary or selective school. Shopping centres are being developed in Edgware Road and in Watling Avenue west of Burnt Oak Station on lands leased by the council.

The majority of the houses will be brick or concrete construction but the scheme includes 464 timber framed houses and about 250 'Atholl' steel houses. When the development of the estate is completed about 3980 houses and flats will have been provided.

The accommodation varies in size from flats of two rooms to houses of five habitable rooms, each of which will be lit by electricity supplied from the Hendon Electric Supply Company Ltd, who have provided the mains and the wiring and the fittings in the houses. Gas is supplied for cooking purposes. The Gas Light and Coke Company Ltd will supply the gas and provide the mains in the road and the pipes and fittings in the houses. The streets are lit by gas.

The rents for the houses vary between 10/- to 17/3d a week.

Wide roads are an important feature of the Becontree Estate

Becontree 1925. General view from 148 Langhorne Road showing foundation walls set out

DEVELOPING BECONTREE

My father worked for the London County Council and he helped to organise the purchase of the land from the farmers for the Becontree Estate. The farmers were very happy with the money they got and most of them were happy about selling. I remember them saying to my father that they were grateful for what he had done and that he had done his duty. They were generous and I can remember hampers of food arriving at Christmas, after they had sold up.

We lived in a very nice farmhouse in Gale Street. The land about us was flat and uninteresting but it was genuine Essex countryside. When we first moved there I had to bicycle four miles to Chadwell Heath Station to get to school. I would pass about four houses and all the fields were growing peas and rhubarb and I used to see the women bundling the rhubarb.

We knew that the construction firms were coming and that we would eventually have to move. They wanted the land that belonged to our house to build a railway station and as the new houses grew up we moved to another Victorian farm house called Burleighs in Chadwell Heath.

My father wasn't highly paid but he had a free house and a car with a chauffeur. I can remember that he often had to entertain visitors from overseas that came to see what was considered at that time, a remarkable project. It was a big estate and my father was quite proud of it and the foreigners thought it was marvellous.

My father then became the Resident Agent for the Becontree Estate. He had to organise the maintenance work and the rent collection. I remember it was very well run and maintained. He was quite happy in his job which was an interesting sociable job and he was supportive in the idea and success of the estate.

Edwin Hardy Amies

Visit by Minister of Health to Becontree, 1st August 1929
Top row from left: L.H. Oliver, Clerk of Housing Committee; Capt. H.W. Amies, Local Resident Representative Valuers Dept. (Edwin Hardy Amies' father); Mr Stevenson, Resident engineer for admin of housing development schemes (Chief Engineer). Front row from left: Mr H.R. Selley, Vice-Chairman of Housing Committee; Mr Arthur Greenwood, Minister of Health; Lord Monk Bretton, Chairman of the Council; Mr E.M. Spence, Chairman of Housing Committee.

King George V and Queen Mary visiting new houses on visit to Becontree, 1923

BUILDING DOWNHAM

I went to work on the Downham Estate in 1925 for the contractor that did the cartage. Our job was to shift ballast, sand and cement, and to pick up the sandbags. We also used to get the job of carting the muck away when the builders cut the footings out.

King George V talking to a bricklayer at Becontree, 1923

Pressing concrete blocks by hand, Becontree. Notice blocks curing in the background

Where Sandstone Road, Grove Park SE12 is now, there were stables and a farm. You had to be at the stable at half past six to get your horse ready and go to the estate. We'd start there round about eight o'clock and finish at five.

The wages were about £2 18s 5d a week, for which you worked damned hard, and when you got home at night you had to clean the horse and put him to bed. And on Sunday mornings you had to go in and look after him.

During the day you would get all sorts of instructions of what to do, twenty-five loads or whatever. You worked on your own all the time, loaded and unloaded your own vehicle and carted it wherever it had to go, sometimes over to the railways, where they used to have train loads of bricks from Hither Green sidings and sometimes to Sandpit Road, where most of the sand and ballast came from.

You used to have all sorts of contractors coming on the estate like the cement people. There was a big cement shed and if you wanted anything you went there and got it. Sometimes you picked up a couple of bags of cement and a bit of sand and took it to a chap working on his own somewhere on the estate.

You only had one horse, unless you had a job where you wanted two or three horses when you'd chain them together. One time we had a big conveyor to move and we had the three horses, one in front of another. Coming up Downham Way was a bit of a job.

We had about twenty to twenty-five drivers and if we wanted extras sometimes we contracted from MacDonalds in Bromley. There were never any strikes on the estate, we didn't know what a strike was and my governor was a pretty decent bloke. I left in 1927 to go to another job working for the local council.

Toby (Downham)

16

My memories of Downham in 1925-6 are of lorries running all over the estate. They were tiny one ton Fords with solid tyres and they used to buzz about through the potholes and ruts. When the lorries came onto the main road they left large dirty muddy tracks. There were also these larger lorries, and their transmission to the rear wheels was a large chain and they used to be very noisy. On the flat part of the estate was a full gauge railway track, and as far as I know there were three steam engines which pulled trucks loaded with bricks.

I can remember the names of two engines, there was 'Puffin' Billy' and the other was called 'London'. They used to run along the bottom part of Downham Way through Rangefield Road and so on but they couldn't go up Southover, it was far too steep there.

John Edwin Smith (Downham)

General view of Downham looking south

LCC's visit to Becontree in 1926 with C.J. Wills train

THE CONTRACTOR'S RAILWAY

C J Wills & Son Ltd, the contractors for the St Helier Estate, faced with the mammoth task of providing material to build a completely new town, decided to construct a supply railway. This they had done before on similar projects at Edgware (Watling) and Becontree.

The railway track of comparatively light weight, was well aligned and ballasted with clinker. It was enclosed with tall chestnut fencing in all public places, and road crossings had proper white barred gates.

They were worked mainly by the train's crew.

Six locomotives worked the line at different times. All were six-coupled, inside cylindered, saddle tank engines and named in order of age: 'Partington', 'Mermaid', 'Woodcroft', 'Edgware', 'Hendon' and 'Lionheart'.

Bulletin of the Wandle Group. June 1981. By J. Williams.

THE TRENCH DIGGER

We lived on the Becontree Estate in Dagenham and as my dad was out of work I had to get a job. My brother-in-law was a gate-keeper on the railway line that carried the building materials onto the estate. It was through his contacts that I was able to get a job as a navvy for C.J. Wills, the local builders. I was employed by them to help dig the trenches for the sewers on the Becontree Estate.

It was still all fields where we were working, though there were railway lines for the building works and the roads had been marked out. There were about thirty people in our team laying sewers, pipes, and digging the trenches, which in those days was all pick and shovel. I got paid one shilling and threepence an hour but I remember the people handling the walling were called the timbermen and they got one penny an hour more. Their job was to put in these big thick timbers and struts which held up the walls of the trench. We could then continue to work without the trench collapsing.

Becontree. Railway track to distribute materials to building plots.

I remember my very first day. I was told by my boss, who was called the ganger, to take a pickaxe out of the tool box. Well of course all the good picks had already been taken by the other workers. The only pick left was a big Anchor and I could hardly lift it, let alone use it. "Never mind," I thought, "I've got to earn some money."

My boss told me to go behind this chap, who was working where there was a line all marked out and I was to start digging down to a particular depth. When it got to four o'clock in the afternoon I could hardly lift myself, and we were supposed to pack up at five! The chap I was working with then said, "Billy pack up, you've done enough for today, I'll clean up the side of the trench for you." When I got home I could have eaten two dinners I was so hungry. I was only eighteen at the time but gradually my muscles got used to the work and I got stronger.

The building site was divided up into sections, each with its own supervisor and ours was called Mr Smithie. He had a vast section. Apart from our team, he had brickies, tilers, plasterers and all other types of trades working under him. He was the boss and you did whatever he told you to do.

After the pipes and sewers had been put in, the builders started working on the houses. They were very quick and you could watch a house going up in front of you. Where there was a plot of land in a field it would be marked out with pegs and string by men in suits. From then on the building of the house was supervised by the Clerk of Works. He would continually come round to see how all the different trades were progressing and check that each trade had done their work correctly. The building would start with the navvies digging out the ground for the foundations.

The foundations or footings as they were called were made to a special formula of sand, cement and shingle. As they were short on labour, I was loaned out to help with this job, which involved mixing and laying the concrete footings. The Clerk of Works would be there to check we had done it properly, always inspecting things were O.K. before the brickies were allowed in.

After the brickies had finished their work, the roof was built. In came the tiler labourers. They had a very precarious job as they used to go up and down those ladders with a load of tiles balanced on their heads. With the outside of the house complete, it was the turn of the carpenters and lastly the gas installers and plasterers.

As it was a vast estate there were hundreds of men working on it. When it was eventually finished, it became the biggest estate in the world. I got used to my job and I particularly liked laying the footings, but after about nine months as a navvy I was unfortunately made redundant. In 1930 there were so many people out of work that all men under the age of twenty-one working for C J Wills were sacked to make way for older men.

I didn't want to leave but I was quickly able to find a job digging for the railway because they were in the process of electrifying the line from Barking to Upminster.

Bill Hahn (Becontree)

18

Roofers at work on Downham. Dennis-Wild houses, 1925

THE HOD CARRIER

A friend of mine who was a ganger told me that his father, a builder's foreman, was looking for a hod carrier to work on the building site of Roehampton Estate.

In those days the only way to find a job like that was by hanging round the boozers or by knowing the right people. I was just eighteen then and looking for work, so I said, "Right," and I got taken on as a hod. I wasn't much interested in the estate and nor was my mother. As long as I had a job, that was all that bothered her. I got paid an hourly rate of one shilling and a farthing. Even though it wasn't that much, it went quite a long way then, and you had to do a nice lot of work for that money.

When I started there were still quite a lot of big fields round the estate. The houses were spread about as only some parts of Dover House had been built.

I was the hod for a team of four bricklayers and two labourers and as I was one of the youngest I was doing really hard work. All the hods were called 'Monkeys' then, so that became my nickname – Monkey!

There was a 'chaser', the governor's right hand man, on site and he was called the 'bellhorse'. The bellhorse was a bloke that got paid a penny extra an hour. He set the pace and did all the leading for the labourers. Whatever the bellhorse did, we had to follow him exactly. Whatever he dropped down, we dropped down too, you couldn't skive nothing and we were chasing our bellhorse up and down that ladder all day long. It was hard work but we had quite a few laughs.

Two brickie teams were needed to build one house and it would take about a fortnight. I remember the bricks being delivered to us by lorry from the London Brick Company. All the estate roads were built before the houses but there was plenty of mud around and ours was a right muddy old job.

All the houses we worked on were built to the same pattern and the brickwork cost about one hundred and twenty pounds. All our houses were really well built and everything had to be just right. There was no skiving and when we had finished a house, we'd just move onto the next site.

Apart from the brickies there were other different teams working on each house. One team did the groundwork. Then someone came and laid the concrete and the footings and then the bricklayers would start, with the scaffolders working round them. Scaffolding in those days was all done with wooden poles, which were just the right length.

Visit the "Atholl" All Steel House

BUILT & FURNISHED COMPLETE WITH ALL BRITISH GOODS.

This All-Steel House is built by The Housing Corporation of Great Britain, 20, St. James Street, S.W., and will remain open for Public inspection from now until DECEMBER 7th, **Daily from 10 a.m. to 5 p.m.**

TAKE TRAM OR 'BUS TO FOOT OF BROMLEY HILL FOR THE "ATHOLL" HOUSE, FURNISHED THROUGHOUT BY CHIESMANS.

Exterior View of The "Atholl" All-Steel House, Downham.
Reproduced by kind permission of "The Daily Graphic."

CONTENTS OF THE "ATHOLL" ALL STEEL HOUSE.

Living Room.

	£	s.	d.
Scotch Made Linoleum Square ... (Kirkcaldy, Fifeshire)	2	12	6
Axminster Hearthrug (made in Kidderminster)		15	0
4ft. Oak Sideboard (made in London)	4	19	6
Oak Dining Table (made in High Wycombe)	5	19	6
2 Oak Adjustable Chairs, 29/11 each (made in High Wycombe)	2	19	10
4 Oak Dining Chairs, 22/6 each (made in High Wycombe)	4	10	0
Oak Mirror (made in Leeds)... ...	1	15	6
6 Pictures (made in Southall) 1/6 each		9	0
Kitchen Kerb (made in Birmingham)		9	6
Combination Dinner and Tea Service (made in Longton, Staffs.)	2	15	0
Room Complete (excluding Curtains)	**£27**	**5**	**4**

P.S.—In this room a perambulator is shown to denote the position intended for it. Price of same is £4 5 0, not included in total cost. Other schemes of inexpensive dining furniture may be seen in our Showrooms.

Scullery.

	£	s.	d.
2ft. 6in. Scullery Table with Drawer (made in London)		15	9
1 Kitchen Chair (made in High Wycombe)		5	9
Mangle (made in Keighley) ..	3	19	6
Towel Roller (made in London)			9
Coal Hod (made in Bilston) ..		3	3
(Not including Blinds, etc.)	**£4**	**16**	**0**

Best Bedroom.

	£	s.	d.
Linoleum Square (made in Kirkcaldy Scotland)	2	12	6
Oak Dressing Chest and Chest Stand (made in London	9	15	0
Bedroom Chair (made in High Wycombe)		7	6
4ft. 6in Oak Bedstead (made in Manchester)	1	19	11
4ft. 6in. Wire Spring Mattress (made in London)	1	10	0
4ft. 6in Wool Mattress (made in London)	1	10	0
4ft. 6in Flock Bolster (made in London		8	11
2 Feather Pillows (made in London)		9	0
Wicker Chair (made in Bridgwater)		15	11
Toilet Set of Ware (made in Stoke-on-Trent)		18	9
Trinket Set of Ware (made in Stoke-n-Trent)		7	11
6 Pictures at 1 6 (made in Southall)		9	0
Oak Mirror		10	0
(Not including Curtains)	**£22**	**3**	**11**

Second Bedroom (Child's Room).

	£	s.	d.
Oak Dressing Table (made in London)	4	19	6
Oak Chest Stand (made in London)	2	19	6
2ft. 6in. Black Iron Combination Bedstead made in Birmingham)		17	11
2 ft. 6 in. Wool Mattress (made in London)		17	6
2 ft. 6 in. Flock Bolster (made in London)		5	11
Bamboo Table made in London) ...		11	9
Linoleum Square (made in Kirkcaldy, Scotland)	1	7	0
2 Pictures (made in Southall) at 1/6 each		3	0
Oak Mirror		10	0
(not including Curtains)	**£12**	**12**	**4**

Third Bedroom.

	£	s.	d.
Grained Oak Combination Chest and Stand (made in London	4	19	6
3ft. 6in. Oak Bedstead with Spring attached (made in London)	2	3	0
3ft. 6in. Wool Mattress (made in London)	1	4	6
3 ft. 6 in Flock Bolster (made in London)		6	11
Feather Pillow (made in London) ...		4	6
Linoleum Square (made in Kirkcaldy, Scotland)	1	7	0
2 Pictures (made in Southall) at 1/6 each		3	0
(Not including Curtains)	**£10**	**7**	**5**

Staircase.

	£	s.	d.
12 Floorcloth at 2/3	1	7	0
Cocoa Mat		5	11
	£1	**12**	**11**

SUMMARY OF CONTENTS
(Curtains extra)

	£	s.	d.
Living Room	27	5	4
Scullery	4	16	0
Best Bedroom ...	22	3	11
Second Bedroom ...	14	14	4
Third Bedroom ...	10	7	5
Staircase and Landing ...	1	12	11

TOTAL
£78 17s. 11d.

Different types of pre-fabricated houses on Downham

The poles were tied together with rope, and they'd be 'as safe as houses'! Scaffolders knew their job. It only used to take them two days, working round the brickies, to rig out one house. Lastly came the roof. Two different contractors were used for that. One for the roofing and one for the tiling.

All the contractors had to carry out the job just right and our foreman was a hard master. He had to be. In them times they had to be hard! Then there were the blokes who would regularly come down to see everything was done right and proper before we could carry on with something else.

Len Dunning (Roehampton)

'Tibbenham' house interior, Bellingham 1926.
Note reproduction Tudor beams

A typical cul de sac (banjo type) on the Watling Estate.
Timber framed non-parlour and Atholl steel
four roomed parlour houses, 1928

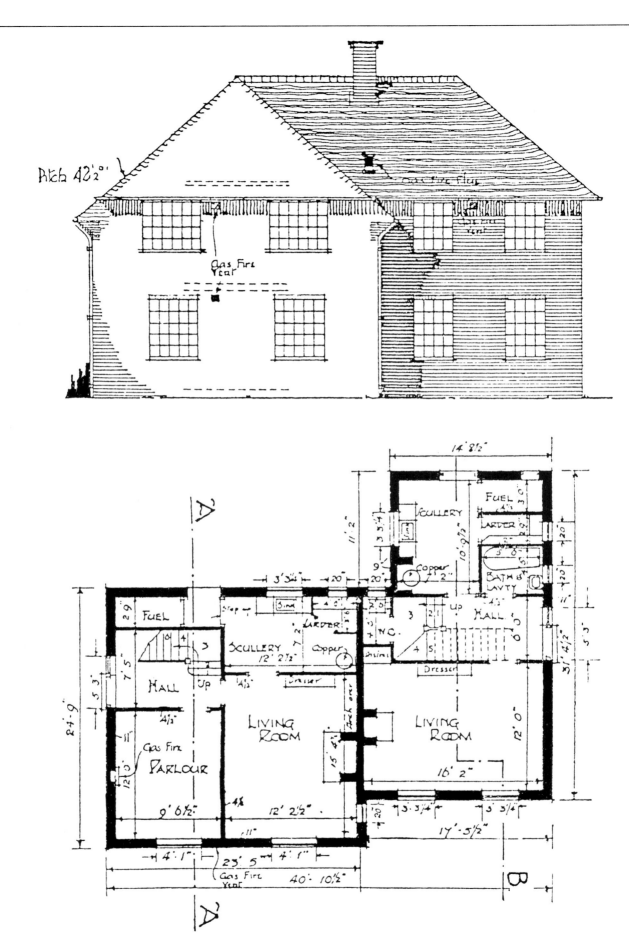

ELEVATION AND GROUND FLOOR PLAN OF END COTTAGES, BECONTREE ESTATE

22

THE MOVE

APPLICATIONS FOR TENANCIES

LCC BECONTREE TENANTS HANDBOOK 1933

Applications for accommodation on the estate should be addressed to the Valuer (Housing) Old County Hall, Spring Gardens SW1.

Applications are generally accepted in the order in which they are received, preference being given to residents in the County of London. At the present time, applications can also be considered from persons living outside the County of London. Persons who are neither living nor working in London can be considered for certain types of houses on north sections of the estate.

Married sons of tenants can be registered for accommodation and married daughters may be registered provided their husbands work in the County of London.

Rents and Accommodation.

The approximate weekly rents (including rates and water charges) are as follows:

Two Roomed Flats	*9/6d a week*
Three Roomed Flats	*11/6d a week*
Three Roomed Cottages	*12/6d a week*
Four Roomed Non Parlour Type	*14/-d a week*
Four Roomed Cottage Parlour Type	*15/6d a week*
Five Roomed Cottage Parlour Type	*17/6d a week*
Six Roomed Cottage Parlour Type	*22/6d a week*

The cottages contain, 3, 4, 5 and 6 rooms (apart from scullery, WC, coal cupboard and bathroom). There are also 2 and 3 roomed flats with kitchens.

Every cottage and flat has a garden, front and back, and is provided with gas, while many have in addition, electricity for lighting.

THE ESTATE CLERK

When I joined the London County Council, slum clearance was being carried out. If council flats were going to be pulled down, people were told of the options that were open to them, Becontree, White City etc. Some people wished to stay right in the East End and if there were new flats going, they would stop there. It was common knowledge that if you wanted to go onto the housing list, there were possibilities of accommodation in whatever area you wanted on the Becontree Estate.

There was an application form to get onto the housing waiting list and it recorded income and any disabilities. The application form would then go through to the central office. I can see it now, 'Valuation, Estates and Housing', and Mr Westwood was the valuer. All people were then interviewed at their home before there was any question of moving. This was done to check domestic standards and to see what the family's financial resources were. It also checked on the size of the family because accommodation was allocated according to how many members there were. For example a couple would be given a one bedroomed flat. A couple with two children of the same sex would have a two bedroomed cottage and so on. If a member of the family suffered from TB, they would then be allocated a separate bedroom. The person carrying out the interview usually had a fairly detailed knowledge of where the family were likely to be accommodated and he could then pass it onto them verbally.

Eric Phillips (Becontree)

A LONG WAIT

My father was a tram conductor and he got all the gen about the estate from the tram depot. In those days you weren't allowed a house unless you could show that you had a regular pay packet, and people like firemen, postmen, bus and tram men got priority, because they had that.

My father asked for accommodation and the council said, "Yes, we will put you on the list, but it may be a long wait." And they came to see where we were living.

Lilian Badger (Castelnau)

As soon as Dad came out of the army from the First World War he put his name down on the waiting list for the Old Oak Estate up at Shepherds Bush. The council wanted to send him to the Becontree Estate down Dagenham but Dad said he wasn't going out that far. You see we were living in Paddington and even Shepherds Bush was a bit of a way.

At the time, civil servants, postmen, bus drivers, bus conductors, people like that who had regular jobs, could get a house quite easily. Dad was a motor coach builder and it was more difficult for someone like him. He'd be out of work for weeks on end, sometimes even long enough to get relief tickets.

Dad used to worry and worry about getting a house so he would often go up to Spring Gardens, Whitehall, where the London County Council had their headquarters. Before he could be given a house, they had to know he would pay the rent. In those days you could be one week behind with the rent but if at anytime you were two weeks late, that was your lot and out you went.

Finally after five years they offered Dad a house in Roehampton. Up till then we had been paying ten bob a week for three rooms in Paddington and when my grandfather heard about the move he had fifty fits and nearly went berserk. He thought Dad was crazy. "How are you going to pay twelve and six a week, and half a crown in rates?" he asked.

My mother was so glad to get away from Paddington. It can't have been easy for her living with her mother-in-law, who was always nagging her, and my grandfather and great grandfather. So when she got this house, with a bathroom and a back garden we could play in and our own front door, she thought she was in heaven.

Ivy Woollett (Roehampton)

I had been on the council list for five years and I was dead lucky to get a house. The council didn't want me to come because I had just moved into such a big room the kids could skate around in it, but my landlady didn't like children and if we wanted a bath we had to go down to the basement and walk through the sitting room of this other flat. I wanted to get out, I wanted a place of my own.

One day someone from the council came to see me. He said, "You're down for a house, but you don't need one." "Oh, but I do." I said. I think he then took pity on me because he said, "You've got two children? Um....". And he kept trying to hint at something but I couldn't think what he was trying to get at. He said, "You don't mind me mentioning this, but if I could say you were expecting another baby, then I could say, yes, the flat is not big enough." "Oh!" I said. I hadn't got the brains to think that one out. But that's how we got down here to Watling.

Elizabeth Knight (Watling)

Aerial view of St Helier, May 1930

24

PRIORITY CASES

In 1934, when I was twelve years old, my family had to leave our flat in Charlton because the property was going to be sold by the owners. As we had nowhere to go, my mother applied to the London County Council to see if they could help. The fact that we would soon be homeless and that I had a history of consistent ill health apparently gave us some kind of priority and my parents were told that they would be given a council house. We were absolutely delighted until we were notified, some time later, that we'd been allocated a house on a new estate being built in St Helier, near Carshalton, Surrey. My parents didn't want to leave London but were too scared to refuse this house in case they didn't get another one. So on the day we moved we were all full of fears about what life would be like in what we thought of as 'The Country.'

Dorothy Barton (St Helier)

When I found out I was pregnant with the second child, my husband went to the council and told them about our circumstances. They said they couldn't get us anything in the same area but if we were prepared to move into one of the newer towns, then they might be able to arrange something.

My husband badgered on at the council and within three months we went over to look at a house. This was very unusual because we'd always understood that it was well over a year or more before you were found somewhere.

Hetty Gates (St Helier)

CHECKING US OUT

I heard about the Roehampton Estate from the office boy at work. Up until then we never knew it existed. We made several enquiries to the London County Council and started getting the Wandsworth Borough News. The council recommended all the other estates but they never told us about the Dover House, Roehampton Estate. It was the best estate and that's why it was so difficult to get into.

The London County Council wanted to know what regiment I was in during the war and if I'd been wounded. You couldn't earn more than four pounds a week and the rent was one pound and two shillings which was much the same as what we were paying for our flat in Pimlico.

Mr Hibbert (Roehampton)

You definitely had to be married to qualify for a house. There were no one-parent families on the Castelnau estate. The estate was for young families.

You couldn't come over here just as a couple, you had to have at least one child, but most people had two children or more.

Mabel Wallis (Castelnau)

CHANGING OUR MIND

The London County Council allocated houses on the Watling Estate to people who lived in the deprived areas in London such as Islington and Camden Town. You will find that nearly everybody that moved there came from that neck of the woods. The East End mob went to the other end of the underground line to Becontree.

My mother's friends moved out of Islington and I think she missed them when they left. I remember she would say, "Oh, yes, I want to come too."

The rent for an estate house was about nine and sixpence and in Islington we paid eight shillings a week. That extra one and sixpence was a terrific lump in those days. People really found it very hard, you know. If they'd come from somewhere in Islington, paying as little as five shillings a week rent, nine shillings was almost double. All the men worked in London and you really had to think about the extra expense of the fares.

I wasn't a very healthy child and where we lived in Islington, we had a place called the 'Medical Mission', where you could get treatment, including your medicines, for sixpence. In those days doctors had to be paid for and there wasn't a clinic on the Watling Estate.

When my mother was offered a house, there was always an excuse not to leave. You see we lived so closely in London, but on an estate you were more spread out and I think people felt they were out in the wilds. Mother had been used to living in a block of flats, a very close community. Watling was way out and Mother was frightened by it.

So when she was offered a house, it horrified her. She was really very frightened of moving to Watling. I think she turned down those houses from the sheer fear of living in the country.

Violet Bunyan (Watling)

We were offered accommodation on council estates but we didn't much like where they were located. We saw blocks of flats where there was hardly a tree in sight. The council always wanted people to go to Dagenham, which was a huge estate. We didn't want to go that side of London at all. We had a friend move there from Battersea, and I went to visit her. She was very happy but I said, "Well, I like your house, but I couldn't live here."

Mrs Hibbert (Roehampton)

A CORNER HOUSE

We were offered a house in Roehampton but my husband, who was a driver on the Piccadilly Line, wouldn't take it. He said he couldn't get to his work in Hammersmith from there, so we were shown a house on the Castelnau Estate, Barnes.

The house was in a street and had a shared path with the house next to it. As I was expecting a baby, I thought with two front doors so close to each other and me getting a pram in and out, it was going to cause trouble. My husband worked different duties and sometimes he came off duty in the early hours of the morning. He wanted his rest during the day and I had to think about the neighbour's children disturbing my husband. So I said to the council that I'd rather have the corner house because it had its own path and they said, "Well, it isn't taken, you can have it if you like." So I had to pay a shilling more in rent for the side entrance.

Mrs Martin (Castelnau)

A double doorway involving shared approach and lobby. Watling 1927

A FIGHTER

People were very envious when we left. They would ask, "How can you get a place when we can't?" They probably hadn't gone the right way about it. We got our house because my mother was a fighter!

Vi (St Helier)

AN EXCHANGE

We came to the Watling estate by what was known as a 'mutual move.' My mother saw this notice in the sweet shop opposite where we were living. A family in Watling wanted to be near Euston Station, as the father worked on the railways. Mother went to look at their house and liked it. The railway worker looked at our flat which was two bedroomed and said, "Oh yes, just what I want." My father, who was a Londoner, was very annoyed about it. He thought going to Watling was like burying oneself in the country.

Amy Ewell (Watling)

WHERE'S THAT?

This letter came to say that we had got a house on the Downham Estate. We had never heard of it. After all those years of waiting we thought we were going to the Burnt Oak Estate, Edgware because it was near Paddington. We had no knowledge we'd ever be going to the border of Kent in South East London. We didn't know that area at all.

Phyllis Rhoden (Downham)

LOOKING IT OVER

In those days you didn't get a chance to view a house on the weekend, you had to view it on certain days. So I came over and they only showed me one house. We fixed the day of the removal and I remember we went to the estate office to get the key. As my husband didn't get any time off work he didn't see the house until he came straight from the office the evening of the move.

Mrs Hibbert (Roehampton)

My mother went to look at the house and when she came back she said it was lovely. We were all thrilled about it. I mean to live up there was like living in Buckingham Palace, compared to what we'd lived in.

Tina Belton (Roehampton)

Before we moved in, we came to the house quite a few times. It was semi-detached and had a small front garden and not a very big back garden. We would sit on the stairs and have our picnic and then wander round. I thought it was smashing really, out in the country. I remember my father said to me, "How would you like to live up here?" And I said, "Oh yes, I like it up here."

Jim Evans (Roehampton)

We lived in Lewisham and as far as I was concerned Lewisham Clock Tower was the hub of the world, I didn't know anywhere else. I was very young at the time, about seven years old, when my father took me by the hand one Sunday morning and we went on an open top bus. I can just remember driving along on through Catford and gradually it became more countrified. We eventually arrived at the bottom of Bromley Hill and it was all very rural.

My father marched me across this wide open space that was all mud and pot holes, and we arrived at this house on the corner of Sandpit Road, so named because there was a sandpit nearby. I was told that it was going to be my new home. I remember the house struck me as being fresh and bright, but what stuck in my memory was the smell of the new cement because there was a concrete floor in the kitchen.

John Edwin Smith (Downham)

arrangements for a removal van to take our stuff from Whitechapel, which was a fair old run you see. Rudge Removals come up to the East End and all there was to move was the bedding, three beds, the china , pots and pans and other bits and pieces. It was very, very rough, because we were very, very poor. Anyway we put what we'd got in this old Dennis removal van and we all travelled with it to Becontree.

George Herbert (Becontree)

The van couldn't get right up to the houses as none of the roads were made up. No tarmac had been laid so we had to carry our furniture from around the corner.

Mrs Martin (Castelnau)

Willetts Removals, Downham

THE REMOVAL BUSINESS

In those days you daren't have the day off for moving because there might not have been a job for you when you went back into work the next day. So Hetty, my wife, packed the lorry and did the whole move by herself.

Alfred Gates (St Helier)

I was pregnant at the time. There wasn't a lot of furniture but we hired a lorry. After we'd seen everything was O.K. in the flat, we left the landlady the door keys because she insisted on having all of them back. We gave the lorry driver instructions of where the house was and I travelled there by train with my girl.

Hetty Gates (St Helier)

Mum and Dad had gone to look around the place in Becontree and there was everybody touting for removing you there. So of course we had to make

Occasionally I would see a furniture van come along and it meant somebody was moving in. We were full of curiosity then and us kids would always dash over to the house and look at who was coming onto the estate.

Ken Wills (Castelnau)

27

People who had moved in perhaps a day or two before you sent round cups of tea. When the next person moved in, my mother would do the same.

Mabel Wallis (Castelnau)

WHAT'S THAT GREEN STUFF?

I was seven when we moved from Kings Cross to Watling. That was back in May 1937. I had never been to the country before and so I had no idea what it would be like. We were told the house was situated near a park and Father said there was plenty of grass. I would dream about parks with grass and roundabouts and swings. I'd seen grass in picture books but I didn't know what it really was so I had to imagine.

We moved to Watling in an old coal van. My father had to help the coalman do some deliveries to get the money for it. I remember it was pouring with rain the day we moved. Mum was in the front of the lorry, and the furniture, along with us kids and Dad, was in the back under a tarpaulin. The journey was about an hour and we was like wet rats when we arrived.

Watling Estate. Road 3, blocks 22/25.
Building in progress, Nov. 1926

As we were brought into the house we thought, "Is this all ours?" I remember saying to my father, "Where are all the other people?" We looked out of the window and my brother who was two years younger than me said, "What's that over there?" He couldn't make out what the green was or what the flowers in the garden were and I was glad he asked because I wasn't sure if the flowers were also called grass.

May Millbank (Watling)

St Helier Estate. Block 940, Sept. 1932

Watling Estate. Montrose Avenue looking north-east, 1926. Railway tracks and building materials

A SEA OF MUD

We had never seen the house before and had no idea what to expect. When we arrived we found a short row of red square boxes all exactly alike and brand new. There were only a few roads built and occupied, surrounded by a sea of mud and great trees lying around waiting to be sawn up and dragged away. Mother and I hated it on sight and she just burst into tears, it was so desolate. But when she found the house had three bedrooms, an indoor flush toilet and a bath in the kitchen, she was reconciled to it.

Dorothy Barton (St Helier)

I DON'T LIKE IT!

We weren't happy about moving in. Coming from a flat to this big house, it was all so strange, so much bigger and different. I think Mum thought, "God, I've got so much now to get on with." Although the council had done it up, it was in rather bad condition. She was so depressed with the house and after the furniture was moved in, Mum was so fed up with herself we just went for a walk.

Daphne Maynard (Castelnau)

I thought our house was all right but my husband didn't like it. To start with he said, "We'll never get our furniture in," and when we moved he refused to do anything. All he did was lay our carpet on the stairs. He didn't even put up the bed. He never spoke to me for nearly two months because he said, "Burying yourself in the country. Nobody's even been past the front door."

Elizabeth Knight (Watling)

IN THE DARK

I had never seen the house before and it was all so strange to us. Mum couldn't find where the gas was to turn the light on, so we sat in the dark until Dad arrived home from work.

Florence Essam (Becontree)

WONDERFUL!

When we arrived, the first thing my girl said was, "Mum can I run up and down the stairs as much as I like?" I said, "You can do exactly what you like, girl." She had a wonderful time up and down those bare stairs, with no carpet or anything. I remember I didn't feel no different about being in a new place except that, somehow or other, it was nice to be able to open the windows and let the fresh air in.

Hetty Gates (St Helier)

I can always remember the first night, it was about ten o'clock by the time we got to bed. We had three bedrooms and when I look at the rooms now they aren't that big, but when we moved in, we thought it was a castle, what with coming from a flat where us five boys had to share one room, you know. It was absolutely wonderful.

Stanley Breeze (Castelnau)

HOUSE AND GARDEN

THE PARLOUR

TUDOR WALTERS REPORT 1918

The desire for a parlour is remarkable both among the urban and rural workers. It is the parlour which the majority desire.

The parlour is needed to enable the older members of the family to hold social intercourse with their friends, without interruption from their children. It is required in case of sickness in the house and it is needed for the youth of the family, in order that they can meet their friends.

It is generally required for home lessons by the children of school age, or for similar serious study, serious reading or writing, on the part of any member of the family.

A parlour is also needed for the occasional visitors, whom it may not be convenient to interview in the living room. It will be seen that considerable importance is attached to the parlour and we consider that whenever possible a parlour should be provided.

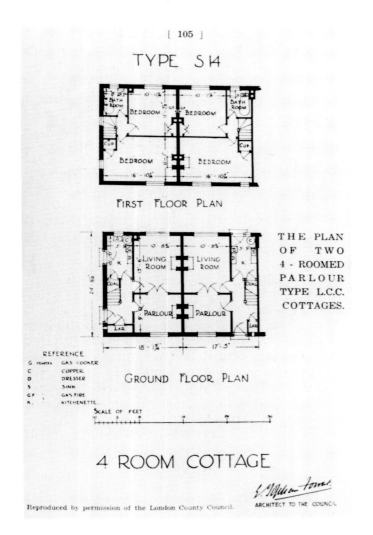

[105]

TYPE S14

FIRST FLOOR PLAN

THE PLAN OF TWO 4 - ROOMED PARLOUR TYPE L.C.C. COTTAGES.

GROUND FLOOR PLAN

REFERENCE
G GAS COOKER
C COPPER
D DRESSER
S SINK
GF GAS FIRE
K KITCHENETTE

SCALE OF FEET

4 ROOM COTTAGE

Reproduced by permission of the London County Council.
ARCHITECT TO THE COUNCIL

We were in what they called a five roomed house, which was three bedrooms upstairs, a toilet and bathroom. We had a 'parlour type' and that was two rooms and folding doors. It was lovely, plenty of room, but once Mum and Dad got settled and there was furniture bought for what we called the parlour, of course that room was never used, except for Christmas or funerals.

Doris Pinion (Downham)

Some of the houses on the estate had two bedrooms and depending how many was in your family some of them had three. Some houses had two living rooms, a kitchen and a scullery, others had a bigger living room and a kitchen.

We all envied people who had what we called the parlour type house because they had an extra room at the front but it was said that all the houses stood in the same area of ground. The parlour type had a narrower kitchen, and their back room wasn't quite as big.

Phyllis Rhoden (Downham)

We had a very small front room which was turned into a bedroom in emergencies. It was too small to use for anything else and when we had company in we'd all have to go to the living room.

Leslie Charles Alder (Roehampton)

PARADISE

It was paradise, we could just look out of my bedroom onto the fields. You could see the flowers growing and there were cows and horses.

Richard (Downham)

NEW FURNISHINGS

I remember my mother going in for this rexine brown suite. It was in the front room and oh, it smelled lovely, you could smell the newness of it, but Mum never let us go in there a lot in case we mucked it up.

Mum had to buy new curtains because all the windows were different shapes then. As my grandfather was a skilled carpenter he made us these big curtain rings.

Florence Essam (Becontree)

BUCKINGHAM PALACE

We'd just got the beds, the four chairs and the table, that's all. So the place was empty. My eldest sister went up to Caledonian Market and bought my mum a big three piece suite, a massive thing, absolutely full of dust. Cor, every time you sat on it, you got a cloud of dust that filled up one room! Then she bought a secondhand sideboard and other bits and pieces, she helped my mum. Then my other sister gave my mum a few bob and we bought some lino floor covering, which was about half a crown a yard in them days. So of course we put it down all over and cor, we thought we were living in Buckingham Palace! We had three rooms upstairs, including the bathroom, two rooms downstairs which had two doors parting them. You could open them out and make one big room. They were big rooms too, and of course to fill them up was a problem, but at least we could fill one room downstairs.

George Herbert (Becontree)

POSH!

When, in 1935, my sister and I started work, things became easier and my mother was able to ease off with the washing that she took in. Holdrons, in Peckham, used to be famous for selling things on the never-never and, in those days, you didn't buy things with cash, you all bought on the never-never.

My mother had aspirations which my dad didn't agree with and she went up to Holdrons and bought a walnut veneer bedroom suite which was like something out of a novel. She also bought, at the same time, a rexine suite with brown velour cushions, a sideboard with twist legs, a square table with four chairs and a rug for the floor. I thought we were posh but Dad was dead against it. I remember his reaction. He yelled and raved and screamed but it made no difference, we still got the furniture. It wasn't the repayments he was worried about, he was just quite content with what we'd

got. He would have spent any amount of money on the garden and allotment, but the home, oh no!

Rosina Evans (Downham)

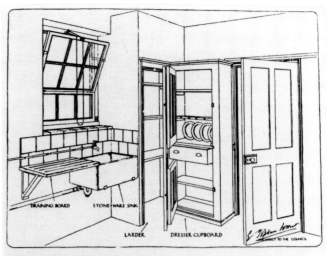

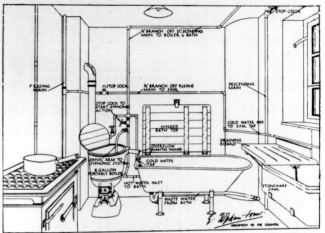

Kitchen fittings of a typical LCC cottage

THE KITCHEN

Inside our houses, each kitchen was complete with an airy larder, a coal fired copper for the washing and the heating of the water, and a large white earthenware sink with a cold water tap. All the kitchens were furnished with a black cast iron gas stove with brass taps, in fact there was quite a lot of brass around. The door handles, pump joints and taps were all kept gleaming and bright with 'Bluebell' at least once a week. The kitchen floor was concrete and the surrounds in the kitchen were cleaned with hearthstone twice a week.

Phyllis Rhoden (Downham)

31

The walls in the kitchen was just like bare brick that had been whitewashed. It was terrible. Kids were not allowed to touch the walls as the whitewash used to come off when you rubbed against it. Every wall had been distempered yellow and you weren't allowed to do anything as regards decorating. In those days the council kept a house empty until it had dried out and they didn't wallpaper because of the cost. There was also the worry about bugs and things like that.

Vera Andrews (Downham)

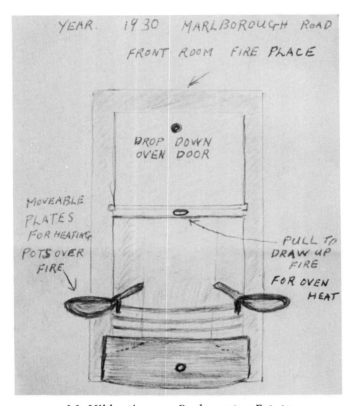

Mr Hibbert's oven, Roehampton Estate

TOTALLY USELESS!

The oven over the fireplace was a great big thing which went almost up the wall, it was so high. The idea was you lit the fire and you could cook in the oven above, but it never worked and no one used them. We used to put our wood in there to keep it dry, or put the washing in to air, otherwise they were an absolute sheer waste of time, totally useless!

Violet Bunyan (Watling)

The fireplace with the oven was in the living room. It was flat with a grill on top, so that you could stand the kettle on it. If you took the kettle off, you could let the top of the fire down, pull a blower and the heat would go up the back of the fire to light the oven above.

Gas was horribly expensive, so we were dependent on coal and that was expensive too. Dad was a motor coach builder and he used to bring spare wood back from his work. In the summer when the weather got hot Mum let the fire go out. But when she cooked the Sunday dinner, she'd light the fire just long enough for the cooking to finish.

Ivy Woollett (Roehampton)

THE PANTRY

As a child I used to read about pantries in books. There would be a picture and it would say, "This is the pantry." I remember I wrote to my friend back in Poplar, "We've got a beautiful house with flowers in the garden, and inside there's a bathroom and a pantry." It sounded so posh!

Florence Essam (Becontree)

THE COAL HOLE

You couldn't cook in the oven because if you put a milk pud in, it used to get smoky. When the oven needed cleaning you had to lift it out and take it outdoors to sweep all the soot off. Oh, it was terrible really.

The other terrible thing in the house was the coal cellar which was under the stairs. I used to dread having the coals in. It was usually delivered in the summer because it was cheaper and we'd get in about half a ton. The coal men would come into the house, with their black sacks scraping the hall walls, and as they turned around, black marks were left behind. Even if you shut all the doors, the whole place wanted spring cleaning, there was dust in the air, everywhere. You'd also get that tarry smell, which came from the coalmen.

Couldn't the builders have put a door in the back yard? Then I wouldn't have had any of that dirt in the house. It was ridiculous.

Mrs Martin (Castelnau)

AN ELECTRIC COOKER

I know my mother was really frightened of the electric cooker and often received shocks from using her old pots and pans which were unsuitable for modern stoves but had been quite adequate for the old black range.

Irene Swanton (Page Estate, Eltham)

NOTE: Although this book is concerned with the LCC estates, we have decided to include a few memories of people who lived on a local council estate (the Page Estate, Eltham, then part of Woolwich Borough). We felt that their memories were of interest and their experiences were very much like those of the LCC tenants.

A.A.

LCC TENANTS TO CHOOSE. `EVENING NEWS'
1927

Downham is entirely a gas lit town and St Helier, the new housing estate is being lit electrically. A new phase was reached today in the completion of gas and electricity undertaking in London. It is true that tenants, with certain exceptions, have not been able to choose which form of heating or illumination they desire.

Formerly the cost to the council for installation of gas or electricity amounted to twenty pounds a house but the cost has been reduced till gas companies are now

prepared to equip the houses free of charge to the council.

Offers have been received to lay the necessary pipes free, on condition that the tenants have freedom of choice. The committee thinks the electricity supply authorities should be placed on the same footing. Both the gas and the electricity companies will be furnished with the names and addresses of incoming tenants and afforded equal opportunity to supply the tenants requirements.

Kitchen, Becontree Estate

The Gas Company was touting for custom when we first moved in. The gas man would knock on your door and persuade you to have gas. You could get a cooker for almost nothing, and if you decided to have gas instead of electricity your cooker came almost free.

Alfred and Hetty Gates (St Helier)

The cookers in those days were supplied by the gas company. You paid fourpence a week for the hire of a gas stove. They were all black stoves and the tops were kept beautiful and clean by rubbing them down with steel wool.

Jim Evans (Roehampton)

It was the first time we had ever had gas mantles and you had to be ever so careful. If you dropped them, they just went to white powder. After about three years the London County Council said they were going to put electric in. You then had to put a penny in the slot and you got about two or three hours. Then the light would go out and you would have to find another penny.

Lilian Beardsmore (Roehampton)

A CLEAN BATH

I remember my first bath in our new house. When we had finished we forgot to take the plug out because we thought the water was to be re-used. When Father said, "The cloth and the stuff is up there to clean the bath up for the next one," we just couldn't believe that each of us could have fresh water. To shut the bathroom door behind me and have a bath in privacy was just heaven.

May Millbank (Watling)

A LOO OF OUR OWN

When we came here it was out of this world. A lavatory, cor, marvellous! Because in them days we never had toilet rolls or anything like that, it was all newspaper. Us kids used to cut the newspaper up into squares and thread it through with string and hang it in the lavatory.

George Herbert (Becontree)

I wanted to go to the loo and I said, "Is anybody in the loo?" Father said, "That loo is ours, just between us." I just couldn't believe it. Back in Kings Cross we shared a communal toilet and for weeks afterwards, I had to think, has it got engaged on the door?

May Millbank (Watling)

THE BEDROOM

You went upstairs and there were three lovely bedrooms. I was very lucky I didn't share a bedroom. I had the smallest bedroom and it was so light, it was lovely. My parents had the front room and my three brothers had the largest back room.

Mabel Wallis (Castelnau)

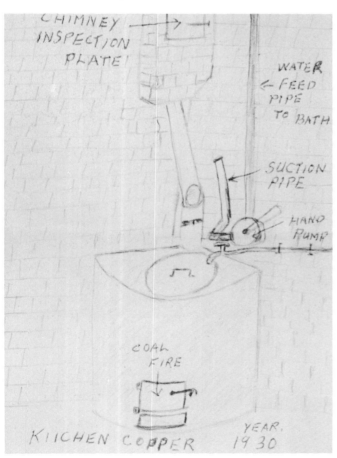

Mr Hibbert's drawing of his kitchen copper, Roehampton Estate

THE BATHROOM

We moved to Roehampton in 1926 and the General Strike was on at the time. The council had finished building our houses in Huntingfield Road, whereas the houses at the bottom of the estate had been done by private contractors. I got to know some pals down there and I went into their houses. They were far better than my parents' house. The houses built by Minters were far more superior, they had a boiler over the fireplace for the hot water and the baths were downstairs. Our boiler was in the kitchen and we had to pump the water upstairs.

Leslie Charles Alder (Roehampton)

A BATH IN THE KITCHEN

There was great excitement when we found that we had got our own bath and could actually get in and fill it up to our necks. My sister and I were quite young and we bathed together and had a lot of fun the first few times, but after that we weren't allowed to waste that much water.

The bath was in the kitchen and when not in use, it was covered by a wooden flap, which then could be used as a table. Under the kitchen window was a deep square sink, fitted with a cold water tap. As this was the only running water in the house, everybody used the sink all the time, from early in the morning, when Dad got up to wash and shave, till last thing at night, when we washed or bathed. In between all this coming and going, Mum had to do the washing up, the laundry, and everything else that needed doing. We all had to be very well organized otherwise there would have been chaos. Anyone going to lock themselves in the kitchen, to have a bath, always had to give prior warning, so that anyone else wanting to use the sink, could do so, while the bath water was getting hot.

I can still see the kitchen window neatly arranged with the household cleaning things on the left and Dad's shaving mug and bristle brush on the right, together with soap in a dish and a nail brush. A narrow roller towel hung behind the kitchen door for drying the hands. We each had our own towel for washing and bathing, and these were hung over the upright ends of the beds.

Dorothy Barton (St Helier)

THERAPEUTIC

I was skinny as a rake and I used to love doing the pump for the bath. It was a lovely exercise and very therapeutic. If for some reason the pump didn't work, which was pretty often, then the hot water had to be taken upstairs by bucket.

Doris Pinion (Downham)

A COLD BATH!

We used to boil up the water for the bath from the gas boiler in the kitchen. As you pumped you had to keep an eye on the gas. We used to put a penny into the gas slot then and you got a good penny's worth. We could have all the baths that we wanted and we found, to our delight, that if our sisters stayed too long in the bath, we could pump cold water from the kitchen into their bath.

Alfred Gates (St Helier)

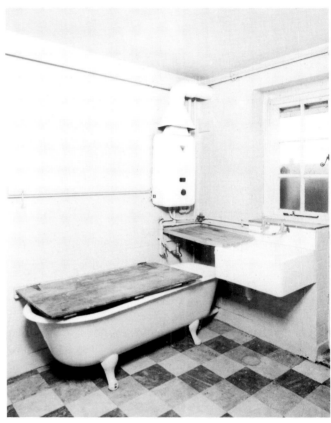

St Helier. View of typical kitchen with bath. Ascot added later. Photo taken 1966

FRIDAY NIGHT IS BATH NIGHT

We were allowed one bath a week, on a Friday night, that was a regular occasion. The bath was upstairs and we would have to pump up the hot water from the coal fired copper in the kitchen. The water used to spurt into the bath through a hole between the two taps. Each pump would send up about two cup-fulls of water so by the time the bath was full enough, it had become cold. In the end my parents finished up by carting the water upstairs in a bucket.

John Edwin Smith (Downham)

IN THE GARDEN

The open effect of grass covered corners. Becontree

GETTING STARTED

We lived on a corner at the end of a terrace. Our front garden was quite big and our back garden was a mere triangle, just enough room to put a few feet of washing line.

When we first moved in there was just a heap of clay in the garden. My father was a foreman bricklayer and I think he got one of the older bricklayers, who was a bit of a gardener, to come and mark it out. I remember him making a circular flower bed and ringing it with lumps of old stone and concrete that had been found among the building materials. I think my father took a few cuttings from the privet hedge and put them each side of the path leading to the front door so that we had a continuous privet hedge all round.

John Edwin Smith (Downham)

On moving into the new concrete, all electric, council house, we found the land behind was a heap of yellow clay, as in the process of digging the foundations and drains, this had been churned up and dumped on the surface, although the ground beneath was formerly fields.

My parents set about developing a garden, something they had never known but had longed for.

Mum was mainly in charge of the operations and it was remarkable what she achieved over the years.

There was a large area of ground, so firstly a crazy paving path was laid made from broken pieces of plaster from the walls of First World War hutments being demolished. Half way along, a rustic arch was erected, which later supported huge bunches of Dorothy Perkins roses in summer. In the right hand centre was a circular rose-bed with fragrant blooms of every colour.

Joyce Milan (Page Estate, Eltham)

COMPETITION TIME

Sunday morning was gardening morning. You'd see people all down the road, in the gardens first thing, digging away. That was their pleasure. Pop would be out there till it got dark and all of us used to give him a hand. I used to cut the grass and trim the hedges and he'd do most of the flowers. The back garden was nearly the same length as the front and oh, it would be lovely sitting out with deck chairs on the grass in the fresh air. It was something different, like going on holiday, it was real nice.

36

7 Oldbury Road, Watling. First prize LCC Garden Competition, July 1931

Joyce Milan with Irene Swanton's sister
in her garden, Downham

A garden competition was started up by the London County Council and each of their estates had a competition of their own. You didn't know when the judges were coming but it was sometime during the summer. Our estate was inspected and judged by the London Gardens Guild and a couple of weeks before the competition, two people from the Guild, with a superintendent and perhaps a surveyor from the council, would come round to look. Once you knew they were on the warpath, you were out there keeping your garden up to scratch and there was great competition amongst us.

Clem, a railway guard at 44 Barnes Avenue, used to take the prizes mostly. He had his garden laid out with concrete paths of diamonds, with crazy paving and all that sort of thing. He had a few bits of grass that didn't need mowing and these narrow flower beds, so he only had a small area to plant out. All he had to do was go down to the market and buy half a dozen potted plants, rather than bring them up from seeds.

As to prize giving, there was nothing like champagne. I think the first prize was ten pounds and a cup, and the other finalists got certificates. To show people who had got the prizes, copies of the certificates were put up in the estate office and as I worked for the council I had the job of sticking them up.

Stanley Breeze (Castelnau)

When my wife and I married, I stayed in the same house. I can't stand gardening but my wife took an interest in the garden and to the neighbours' surprise we won a London County Council second prize for the front garden, which was ten shillings. When the judges came to give the prize they said, "Are you new people here?" "No," I said, "I've lived here all my life." "Well, what's happened to your garden?" "My wife, she loves gardening," I said.

Jim Evans (Roehampton)

43 Gaskarth Road, Watling. Prize garden, July 1929

THE GARDENING CLUB

After I left school I worked on the estate as a plumber for the council and before the war started my supervisor, who liked gardening, said, "Do you think you and your Pop could set up a gardening centre on this estate?" Well, we had a meeting and my supervisor decided we needed a shed to trade from, because we weren't allowed to trade from the council yard on a Sunday morning. After a couple of weeks he managed to get hold of this big shed and we had it put next to the church hall in Stillingfleet Road. We then got a notice all round the estate that the gardening club had opened.

For the first couple of months I was put in charge of receiving the goods, which were delivered into the council yard. Naturally we used to buy in bulk and the big lorry came with the lime and pots and other things and I'd check it over. On Sunday at eight o'clock we'd take the goods to the shed, which took a bit of carrying. We'd weigh up the lime into seven pound bags, organise all the boxes of plants and get everything ready for when we opened, from ten o'clock to twelve o'clock. The things at the club would be about tuppence a pound cheaper than in the shops, which in those days was a lot. We wasn't allowed to make a profit and we didn't want to, we were just there to help the people.

Stanley Breeze (Castelnau)

Everyone was new to gardening and you learnt from scratch. A little gardening club started up just for the estate and you could buy plants and anything else you needed at cost price. If you had something to sell or exchange, you could put a little note up. I had an allotment to grow vegetables, and we paid a very small rent for it, but you got your money back on it. At the club there was a shop where people could exchange vegetables and lend each other things.

Violet Bunyan (Watling)

A BLAZE OF COLOUR

My mother was mad on flowers, she was a real garden lover. Her flower garden in front of the house was a joy to behold and I doubt if she ever bought a plant. Different neighbours gave her cuttings and roots and she grew a beautiful privet hedge by this method.

You were allowed to do anything you liked with your garden as long as you kept it nice. All the gardens on the estate were nicely tended and some were excellent. We had garden competitions but we didn't go in for any because it wasn't my mother's way of gardening.

Phyllis Rhoden hedge cutting in Launcelot Road, Downham

We used to buy penny packets of seeds and get our bean poles from a nursery off Burnt Ash Lane, Bromley. Mr Prior was the nursery man and it was really lovely going there and seeing all the plants growing. From our seeds we grew mignonettes and little tiny black violas and we had hundred of flowers. Mother would gather rocks from heaven knows where and she grew her Snow on the Mountain, London Pride and ice plants around them.

Our roses were the old fashioned kind, deep pink cabbage roses, with the most beautiful perfume. There were quite a few houses that were being knocked down around our way and we used to go to their gardens and bring an old rose tree home. We had large marguerites in June, and the tall single sunflowers were very attractive. One occasionally saw the big plate, eight foot sunflowers, but these were regarded as curiosities, with their habit of turning their faces to follow the sun. The daddy-long-legs made their home there and apparently preferred to live at the back of the blooms. My favourites were the hollyhocks which thrived under the plum tree and around our windows. They always spelled home to me.

The well-tended gardens were all part of the scene and in summer were an absolute blaze of colour. No one moaned about the grass cutting and those were the days of non-electric garden machinery. It was all part of the joy of having your own patch.

Phyllis Rhoden (Downham)

Joyce Milan with her father digging in their garden, 1930s

Becontree garden

Every inch of the garden was used, growing flowers of every kind. I cannot recall any flower my mother had not attempted to grow at sometime. She could take a cut flower, put it in the earth, and it would grow. Many delightful chrysanthemums were produced this way. I fear I never inherited the gift.

Beyond the gate, we grew vegetables of all kinds, potatoes, carrots, cabbage and Brussels sprouts. Even celery and cucumbers were given a try. Mum planted a small apple tree which produced delicious fruit, and recently I peeked over the nearby church wall to look at our garden and was pleased to see the same tree, now grown very large, in the same spot.

Also to add to our pleasure, we had a small aviary of singing canaries near the house.

Our garden was always a blaze of colour in the summer months, with neighbours often calling at the door requesting that their friends or relations could view, there not being much profusion of flora in Inner London areas in those times.

We never took a holiday, mainly due to lack of money, but even in later years after I had married, my mother considered she had everything in the garden and did not need holidays elsewhere. She always felt she had her own bit of country on that council estate.

Joyce Milan (Page Estate, Eltham)

Downham family in their garden

ESTATE MANAGEMENT & MAINTENANCE

RULES AND REGULATIONS

CONDITIONS OF TENANCY FOR THE CASTELNAU ESTATE 1930-33

1   *The total weekly rent shall be paid in advance each Monday to the Superintendent at the Estate Office.*

2   *THE TENANT SHALL NOT:*

(a) *Assign this Agreement either in the whole or in the part.*

(b) *Underlet the premises or any part thereof.*

(c) *Use the premises or any part thereof as a shop or workshop, or for the carrying on or the storage of the implements of any trade or business.*

(d) *Expose in the premises or any part thereof any goods or materials for sale or hire.*

(e) *Drive nails or allow or permit nails to be driven into the walls of the premises.*

(f) *Allow or permit pictures to be hung otherwise than on picture rails, when provided by the Council or on picture hooks of a pattern supplied or approved by the Council.*

3   *THE TENANT SHALL NOT without the previous written permission of the Council:*

(a) *Affix to or exhibit on the premises any notice, nameplate or advertisement.*

(b) *Keep on the premises or any part thereof any pigs, rabbits, fowls or pigeons.*

(c) *Erect or permit to be erected any structure in the garden of the premises.*

(d) *Erect or permit to be erected any wireless aerial or make any attachment to the premises in connection therewith.*

(e) *Accommodate lodgers.*

4   *THE TENANT SHALL keep the front garden of the premises in a neat and cultivated condition, and shall give the Council's staff reasonable facilities for maintaining and cutting the hedge abutting on roads.*

5   *The tenant shall be entitled to use the back gardens of the premises as a drying ground for his own washing, but shall not otherwise expose to public view or hang out from the windows or on the balconies of the premises any washing or any unsightly objects.*

6   *The tenant shall in his turn, as determined from time to time by the Superintendent, keep any passage, staircase or yard that he shares with other tenants swept and clean. He shall also, in a like manner, light and extinguish any lamp used to light a staircase, passage or yard.*

7   *The tenant shall deposit refuse from his premises in the dustbin provided by the Council and shall in all other respects observe the arrangements made from time to time for the collection of refuse.*

8   *The tenant shall clean the windows of the premises at least once every week.*

9   *The tenant shall have all chimneys in use swept at least once every year.*

10 *The tenant shall immediately after any birth, case of infectious disease or death occurring in the premises, report the same to the Superintendent at the Estate Office.*

11 *The tenant shall on the occurrence of any case of infectious disease in the premises cause the person affected therewith to be removed at once to a proper hospital.*

12 *The tenant shall give the agents and workmen of the Council (and of the local authority if so required by the Council) all reasonable facilities for entering upon the premises at all reasonable hours in the daytime for the purpose of inspecting the state and repair thereof and of doing such repairs thereto as may be considered necessary and of seeing that the conditions of this Agreement are being observed.*

13 The tenant shall repay to the Council the cost of any *special cleaning* necessitated on the determination of the tenancy by reason of having left the premises in a dirty condition.

14 The tenant shall repay to the Council the cost of repairing any *damage* done to the premises (other than that resulting from ordinary fair wear and tear), and of clearing stoppage in drains due to carelessness.

15 The tenant shall repay to the Council the cost of replacing *windows* broken in the premises during the tenancy.

16 The tenant shall sign an acknowledgement of the number of *keys* supplied to him at the commencement of the tenancy, and pay the sum of five shillings as representing the value of the said keys. He shall be entitled, on the determination of the tenancy, to a refund of the balance of the said sum of five shillings, remaining over after the Council have applied any part of the said sum in or towards the cost of replacing the keys lost or not handed over to the Council or in or towards rent not paid in or towards the cost of repairing damage done to the premises by the tenant or in or towards any other expenses payable by the tenant.

17 The *tenancy may be determined* by the Council at any time by seven days notice in writing.

On breach by the tenant of any of these conditions, the tenancy may be summarily determined by the Council at any time.

The tenancy may be determined by the tenant at any time by seven days' notice to expire on a Monday, signed by the tenant and given to the Superintendent at the Estate Office.

18 The local *rates*, house duty and water rate paid by the Council for the period current at the date of entry into occupation are equal to the weekly sum charged to cover payment for the same. In the event of the local rates and water rate being either increased or decreased the Council will give or cause to be given to the tenant seven days notice in writing of the said increase or decrease and of the consequent alteration in the amount of weekly rent payable by the tenant and of the date from which such alteration will take effect and the total weekly rent payable shall be increased or decreased accordingly.

THE INSPECTORS ARE COMING!

When we first moved to Downham we had inspectors every so often to come and see if you were keeping the place clean. The word would go round, the inspectors are coming!

When you moved you had loads of rules to keep. The windows had to be washed every fortnight and the front step cleaned once a week. No mats were to be shaken after ten o'clock. No cats, no dogs, no pets of any kind. Then indoors there used to have to be a fire guard for the children. You had to keep your children under control at all times, you couldn't let them run about and do as they liked. They couldn't go on the greens or climb trees or anything like that.

If you didn't abide by the rules in the rent book, you'd get a real severe letter from the council. They didn't give you many warnings and they'd take action against you. Same with the children. They'd send for you to go up to the council office if someone reported your children misbehaving or misusing the greens, anything like that.

Beatrice Kitchen (Downham)

No. **F 3476**

London County Council.

VALUATION, ESTATES AND HOUSING DEPARTMENT.

Received of Mr. _J.W. Chapman_ a

deposit of _FIVE_ shillings and _——_ pence

in respect of the tenancy of No. _75 Headcorn Rd_

Dated this _14th_ day of _June_ 19 _27_.

J.W. Clark

for Superintendent. }
~~Caretaker.~~

NOTE.—The deposit is held as a guarantee that the tenement will be handed over in a good and clean condition, and deductions will be made therefrom for any keys missing or any unsatisfactory condition of the tenement or fittings due to the tenant's carelessness or neglect.

The deposit will not be refunded except on production of this receipt.

One of the rules of the estate was to keep the front garden looking nice. The council caretaker would look at the front gardens and if yours was out of order, or well and truly overgrown, he would knock on your door and say, "You must get this front garden cleaned up and I'll come and see it in a week's time." You were given that week to get it tidy or you were in trouble.

The caretaker had his own estate house and he used to cycle round the estate twice a day, morning and afternoon. If the children were doing anything they shouldn't, they would run away as if he were a policeman coming.

Lilian Badger (Castelnau)

THE GREENS

Children weren't allowed to swing on the gates or play on the greens. You were allowed to go on the paths and that was it. There used to be a chap going round the streets, we called him the Green Man. He was very strict and would chase us off the greens. He used to say, "You've got back gardens to play in." He kept the estate in good order and it didn't get vandalized, as the children were frightened of him. As soon as we saw him on his bike, we used to run.

Florrie Abel and Gladys Hanson (Bellingham)

Children weren't allowed to play on the greens, lean on the hedges or kick footballs around and if they did, 'Happy', as we called him, who worked for the council, was the one to say, "Get off there!" The children respected him and they called him 'Happy' but he was a bit solemn really.

Mrs Hibbert (Roehampton)

On the corners of most roads was a little green which was surrounded by wooden stakes with a metal pole connecting them together to form a low fence. Everyone called them 'the greens' and they were regularly trimmed once a week. We weren't really supposed to play on them, but we did. I remember there was one man who used to go berserk when anybody used to go on the green. He had one leg and of course he was called 'Peg Leg', and he was a right miserable old bugger!

We used to play cricket on the green and it was very unfortunate but if the ball was going to go through anybody's window, it always went through one particular woman's window. Of course in the end she got so incensed that she used to keep the balls. The local policeman would come round and sort it out. We would probably end up with a clip round the ear, but he'd get the balls back for us. Later on we would find our pocket money had been docked to buy a new window.

Ken Wills (Castelnau)

Watling Avenue showing Virginia creeper over frontages

A PRETTY ESTATE

Watling was a lovely clean estate and very pretty. The council had planted all this five-fingered-Jack, that's Virginia Creeper, and every house was covered in it. It turned brilliant red in the autumn, the colour of a beetroot plant and it looked absolutely beautiful. The council used to come round twice a year and trim the leaves round the windows but of course they found it too much hard work and in the end it was mostly dug up. If you walk around the estate today you can still see a little of it left.

People from the council would come round and cut everybody's hedges and the lawns in the cul-de-sacs, not just the bits that showed on the main road. They'd encourage people to keep things nice. Keepers would go round and you never got children breaking things down, probably because they were a bit more frightened of authority.

Violet Bunyan (Watling)

NO PETS ALLOWED

I thought the house was smashing but the only thing that upset me a bit was that you couldn't have any pets up here. No pets whatsoever were allowed by the London County Council. Back in Regents Park where we used to live, we had a big black rabbit that was almost wild. It used to run round the garden and chase the cats, and he had to be left behind.

Jim Evans (Roehampton)

THE ESTATE OFFICE

I saw this advertisement by the London County Council's Valuation, Estates and Housing department in the News Chronicle Newspaper. It was for Estate Clerks, and said, "A knowledge of building methods would be an advantage." I applied for the form and I remember it had about four blank pages for you to write about your experience in building. As I didn't have very much at all, I just put the word 'slight' on the first page and on the subsequent pages I said, "See page one."

Of course I got the inevitable answer, "Thank you for your application but at the moment....etc." But twenty-four hours later it was followed by another letter which said would I please arrange to come for an interview.

The sub-committee of the Housing Committee interviewed me. They were rather helpful as I was a delegate to the London Trades Council and had got the secretary to stand as a referee. The other referee was my trade union organizer and as it was a Labour run council it went down fairly well.

Downham Estate Office, Headcorn Road, 1927.
Note LCC classes sign

A letter then came to say I had been appointed as an Estate Clerk on the Becontree Estate for the princely sum of two pounds and ten shillings a week. It was December 1937 and I was just twenty-two years old.

That first Monday, I had to report at half past nine in the morning to the Estate Office at 100 Ford Road. I got there early and was met by the Superintendent of the section who was a lovely gentleman and he made me most welcome. We went inside the office, at twenty past nine, with the office due to open at half past. There was another clerk there and the superintendent showed me what I had to do. He said, "There's the rent book and there's the squares with the dates against them. You put down the amount and you enter it on a sheet of paper, which is headed with the name of the road. You put the number of the house and the amount you've taken. There's five pounds worth of change over there, sort it out in the till here." Then he said, "Oh, I've got to open the office now." And that was the extent of my training.

Becontree was divided up into twenty-one sections with an estate office in each one of them. The rent offices were graded from 1 to 4, with 4 being the smallest. I worked in a Grade 1 which consisted of a Grade 1 Clerk, two estate clerks and a Superintendent who lived in a cottage adjacent to the office. Some Superintendents had accommodation, a flat over the office.

We would take 800 rents every week. At the end of the week we then did a balancing trick with the figures, put it down on a sheet of paper and sent it up to the central office at 882 Green Lane, Dagenham.

There was an iron grille between me and the customers and they would push their rent book and their cash underneath the grille. The grille was there so if anyone got irate about something, they couldn't jump at you over the counter. If there wasn't much of a queue, one or two people would have a chat with me. A very few were abusive but otherwise the people were reasonable and I think we were too.

In the afternoons we executed new lettings, that was when someone would come along and view a cottage. Most of the people took what was offered them. You issued them with a rent book, and there was a five shilling key deposit, which was refundable if they moved out providing five shillings worth of damage, for instance broken windows, had not taken place.

Another job we had to do was serve notice to quit. If people were a week in arrears with their rent, we would send a 'First Arrears Letter', which would be a gentle reminder. If it continued for another two or three weeks, you would send a second letter of rather sterner stuff, "Look here, you've got to pull yourself together and get paid up, or else!" If there was no effort being made you would serve a notice to quit. This was merely a safeguard just in case it went on and on and on. If the rent didn't get paid they would end up in court.

As I recall there were a very few actual evictions during my couple of years before the war. Usually the family would skeddadle, leave without giving their notice. Possibly there had been a family dispute or he or she fancied the bottle too much or had got into debt on the horses, having used the rent in order to back the next winner that lost!

Eric Phillips (Becontree)

PAYING THE RENT

We moved to Dagenham from a two bedroomed flat in Bromley where the rent was four shillings and five pence a week. In Dagenham it was expensive, the rent was fifteen shillings and two pence. Well we wanted the house, we had to manage.

Amelia Cogley (Becontree)

Mr. Peardmore — The Net Rent is **15/6** per week, and the balance payable represents the charge to cover payments for local rates, house duty and water. — No. **13 HUNTINGFIELD ROAD.**

| Due Date. | Cash Received. | | Initials of Receiver. | Due Date. | Cash Received. | | Initials of Receiver. | Due Date. | Cash Received. | | Initials of Receiver. | Due Date. | Cash Received. | | Initials of Receiver. |
	Date.	Amount.			Date.	Amount.			Date.	Amount.			Date.	Amount.	
1921. Mar. 21				1921. June 20				1921 Sept. 19	19/9	23/6	CH	1921. Dec. 19	19/12	23/5	CH
28				27				26	26/9	23/6	CH	26	26/12	23/5	CH
Apl. 4				July 4				Oct. 3	3/10	23/6	CH	1922. Jan. 2			
11				11				10	10/10	23/6	CH	9			
18				18				17	17/10	23/6	CH	16			
25				25				24	24/10	23/3	CH	23			
May 2				Aug. 1				31	31/1	23/3	CH	30			
9				8				Nov. 7	7/11	23/3	CH	Feb. 6			
16				15				14	14/11	23/3	CH	13			
23				22				21	21/11	23/3	CH	20			
30				29				28	28/11	23/3	CH	27			
June 6				Sept. 5				Dec. 5	5/12	23/3	CH	Mar. 6			
13				12	2/9	22/6	CH	12	12/12	23/3	CH	13			

N.B.—The rent is due on Monday between 9.30 a.m. and 1 p.m. for the week commencing that day.

Because there was no social security in those days the council had stipulations on our estate that one had to earn at least three pounds, ten shillings a week, so that you could afford the rent. As the houses were built for the working class, the maximum you could earn was five pounds. The rent my mother paid for a four roomed cottage was twelve shillings and sixpence. The rates, were half a crown, and it brought it up to fifteen shillings a week.

Leslie Charles Alder (Roehampton)

TOO WELL-OFF TO BE A COUNCIL TENANT

There was one friend of mine whose father was a bus driver. With his overtime and his basic wage he got just under five pounds a week. Well it came to the ears of the London County Council that this man ran a private dance band, so he got six months notice to move off the estate, which might have done him a lot of good because he bought his own house.

Leslie Charles Alder (Roehampton)

HARD TIMES

When they had a big strike over at Fords my husband was out of work for three years. All we got was three shillings labour money, a loaf of bread and blue tickets. I can see them tickets now. I used to hate going into the shop with them. But we stuck it through.

We paid our rent weekly and the same rent collector used to come round and knock at the door. A lot of people, if they didn't have the money, wouldn't open the door. There must have been quite a lot of people on the estate who couldn't afford the rent and I imagine the pawn shop was pretty busy. I had to pawn my husband's boots and his chain. I done that because I'd lost a baby and wanted her buried and I never could get that chain out again.

Betty Mapstone (Becontree)

The total rent we paid was fifteen and six. Mind you, that was for a three bedroomed house. I had to pay five shillings for the keys and I got a key to every door including the coal cellar and the broom cupboard. I've still got my keys and I don't know what the council would say if I took them in now!

Vi (St Helier)

THE THREAT OF EVICTION

The rent always came first then and my mother always knew what time the rent collector was coming and it was jam and toast for a couple of days after the rent had been paid. My parents used to say, "Right, we have got X amount for food and if there is any money spare, one of you can have a pair of shoes." But the rent always came first.

If you didn't pay the rent you were given a month to move out, irrespective of whether you'd got one or ten children, you was out! I think if a family had to leave, they'd be put in a halfway house. There used to be one up at the Edgware General Hospital.

It looked like a block of flats and they had communal eating there. People would stay there until such time as they had pulled their socks up. But you never saw the same people back on the estate again.

May Millbank (Watling)

As a kiddie I remember wanting to know why some people had their furniture put outside. I would come home from school and sometimes see people being put out of their house by the council and I would feel sad. If it was raining, a kind neighbour might come out with a bit of tarpaulin to cover the belongings. I'd ask my mother about it and she'd say, "Those people couldn't pay their rent, so the council have put them out." And I suppose those that couldn't afford the rent went to a relative.

Florence Essam (Becontree)

REPAIRS, PAINTING AND DECORATING

Behind our office was a yard which had a carpenter, a plumber, a handyman and a few decorators. People would come in reporting repairs to us and after we had balanced up in the afternoon, we would issue chits for the workmen. Usually there was quite a lapse between asking for a job to be done and it being executed because demand exceeded the human resources to meet it.

Another job we had was to show people the wallpaper book which had about half a dozen patterns in it. If a house was due for decoration they could choose which wallpaper they wanted. The Grade 1 clerk was then responsible for issuing the instructions to the decorators and he would make out a schedule.

I was on probation for the first year and after that it was the beginning of my forty odd years with the London County Council and the Greater London Council.

Eric Phillips (Estate Clerk, Becontree)

Repainting on Downham

I left school at fourteen and got a job on the council. I had no intention of working for them but the superintendent of our estate said to my Father, "How would your son like to come and work on the council? He can learn all the trades, and it will be alright for him later on."

I wasn't over keen but the estate office was next door to where I lived and the job was worth fifteen shillings a week and I thought, "Fifteen bob, that sounds nice. Yes that sounds alright." So I gave it a try.

Joe Thompson was the estate handyman and I went out with him.

Perhaps we'd mend a few waterways but as time went on we had to have a plumber for the big plumbing jobs. Anyway this fellah, Mr Green, came along and from then on I was the plumber's mate. Because he was on call all day he managed to get a house on the estate.

As council employees we didn't just work on the estate but also went to White City, Old Oak Common, Tooting and Hamble estates. We also looked after the fire stations which came under the council.

Naturally as the estate established itself, more men came to work in our office. Every estate had their permanent staff. You had your fitter, bricklayer, plasterer, plumber and they all had their mates except for the carpenters.

It really wasn't bad working, and I liked mucking around. I remember many a time I used to listen to the wireless, and when the time signal went at eight o'clock I'd jump out of bed and dash to work. The first thing we'd do was to have a cup of tea. Then you'd have your jobs, which might be a tank overflowing, the usual thing. We'd go round and repair that. Then perhaps, come dinner time, the bricklayer or plasterer had a special job, so they'd say, "Oh, I shall want a mate this afternoon," and it would be, "Oh, go and see about it Stan." So that afternoon I'd be the plasterer. Then the following day maybe a floor needed to be taken up and someone needed a carpenter, so I'd give a hand.

If there were any complaints, the superintendent used to go round and, if he couldn't get any satisfaction, he would fetch the surveyor down. The surveyors would come round and they used to poke their nose in on us. There was this one little fellah, I will call him Mr X, anyway he was one of those, you know, just out of college. I don't suppose he was more than twenty-one but he'd find fault with everything.

I remember one day I was over at a house, doing some repairs and there was a decorator working there. The property we were working on was damp so Mr X comes along, pokes his head through a window and says to the decorator. "Do you think it would make a difference if you made your paste with self-raising flour instead of ordinary flour?" And that was Mr X!

In those days the houses were papered every five years. The distemperers and paperhangers would come in and I might go and give them a hand because I wanted to know how it was done. The insides of the houses were painted in yellow ochre and the bedrooms done up in distemper.

Distemper was a mixture of whitewash and size. The whitewash used to come in lumps of chalk. It was put into a bucket, water was poured on to it and it was then left for a day. Concentrated size was then mixed up with hot water and poured into the whitewash and this would make it stick onto the wall. The stock colour, a yellow ochre powder was then added to the mixture and that was the only thing the council had on the inside walls. I remember the yellow ochre used to come in 28lb bags and, many a time, you'd go to pick up the bag, and it would split everywhere. The ceilings were painted white, and the decorator used to put a little bit of blue in with the ordinary white, as it made it look nice.

The council also had their own painting gang of about twenty to twenty-five painters, and they used to go from estate to estate. Practically all the external paint work was white except for the front and back doors which were done in Brunswick green. The decorators used to put varnish over the paint which gave it a lovely beautiful finish and when the front door was done over it used to look very nice.

Working for the council was a good job as I got to know all the trades, saw all the houses and I knew practically everyone on the estate. I worked at Castelnau for a couple of years but then the council wanted someone on the Roehampton Estate and I was transferred over there. The thing that got me down about that place was the hills.

Stanley Breeze (Estate Worker, Castelnau)

DECORATING – THE TENANTS' VIEW

About every five years the council came to decorate the inside of your house from top to bottom. There was a choice of two colours, buttercup yellow and pale green, and the paint was always a sort of beige, pastry colour.

The decorators would be there about a week and you were expected to be prepared for them. They would say, "We want the top front bedroom on Monday," and you were expected to have that room cleared right out. They did the stairs, the kitchen, the bathroom and so on and we weren't allowed to have any wallpaper then. I don't know why. The front and back door was always painted green and it wasn't until after the war they started doing the doors different colours.

Lilian Badger (Castelnau)

When the council did the decorating, you did get a choice of wallpapers. They had a book and you chose whichever pattern they had. But if you didn't like any of their patterns and wanted to go out and buy your own paper you could, the council still put it up for you. Most people waited for the council decorators because they really couldn't afford to pay out for paper and paint. In those days people had just about enough money to carry on without the extras, you know. Eventually things changed and everyone started decorating to their own taste.

I remember there was an argument between a friend of my mother and the decorators. She had paid a lot of money for a pink, silk-stripe effect, regency wallpaper, it was rather nice. I remember she was in a real state about it, saying that the decorators hadn't put it on straight.

Phyllis Rhoden (Downham)

SETTLING IN

WE LIVE IN THE COUNTRY

When we came to Dagenham we had fields and plenty of fresh air. Most of the fields round the yard were pea fields, cabbage fields and all that. When the word got round that it was being bought up by the council for building, we were allowed to go and take what was there. I'd get the pram out and load it up with cabbages. My mum would say, "Go and fetch us some rhubarb or peas."

There was an orchard on the other side of the railway and I can remember getting the pears. Me and Emmy, my sister, would listen for the train, "No trains coming." We'd cross over and climb up, get those pears and take them home.

There was a little stream near us and we used to dam it up with mud and bricks, anything we could find. It got deeper on one side so that we could paddle. It was lovely then. We used to get some sausages and potatoes off my mum and we went over to where the trees were. Emmy and I used to build a little fire, put our potatoes in and cook the sausages on a fork. We used to smoke the sausages dirty but we enjoyed them.

Florence Essam (Becontree)

Dagenham Road, Becontree.
Site of 'Farnham Tavern', 1930s

DOWN ON THE FARM

We moved to a house opposite a farm and the farmyard went straight across the road, as a matter of fact you could just step over a ditch and be in the cabbages. Compared to the closeness of the East End, it was country you know, the spaciousness of Downham, it was absolutely beautiful.

Ron Chattington (Downham)

Ivy Woollett's mother and father, Roehampton

SHOWING OFF

When I was about twelve, another girl and I rode our bicycles all the way back to our friends in Westminster, just to show off that we lived in the country. We tried to put on country accents and pretended that we lived near a farm and had to go to school across a railway line. Mind you, we didn't tell them that the school was only across the building line. And do you know our friends were open-mouthed listening to us. Looking back on it, it was so silly but you know kids.

Vi (St Helier)

Block 433 Muchelney Road, St Helier, 1931

NEW NEIGHBOURS

When you get in the country it's different. I mean the people, they're complete strangers to you, you don't know where they're from and they're just as suspicious of you as you are of them. It takes quite a long time to break down the reserve of some people. Some people can mix easily, others can't.

Mr Brooke (Becontree)

People came from different places and parts of the country, and they were all a different class of person. You'd get some from a rough neighbourhood and some from a decent neighbourhood.

Stanley Breeze (Castelnau)

When the people and their children moved on to the estate they were virtually in the same age group. They were all young and just starting with their families. As far as I know the whole population lived in harmony. We had all sorts, butchers, bakers, candlestick makers.

Ken Willis (Castelnau)

I've always been a self-sufficient person. When we moved to St Helier I didn't really miss my mother because I think with having the children and my own home it made a difference. My mother lived in Deptford and she came to see us a couple of times and just once in a while, we used to go down by tube and see her. The tube was very useful because I could connect at the Oval and get a bus through to Deptford.

We got friendly with our neighbours very quickly indeed. As it was a new estate most of them had only been there three years when we moved. They told us where the shops were and everything else about the estate.

Hetty Gates (St Helier)

Eaton Gardens, Becontree 1927. Typical banjo road layout on garden city lines

HE'S A DECENT BLOKE

Well, I think the friendliness amongst the people in Dagenham was because they were all working class people. They all had to do manual work for their wages. They all realised that they could all have the same kind of trouble come to them. They just looked at the chap next door and they said, "Well, he's a decent bloke, he works hard. He goes out early in the morning, comes home late at night." Because we were all in the same class, you got that friendliness.

Anonymous (Becontree)

BACK TO THE OLD HAUNTS

There were quite a few families that came on the estate that never settled and they agitated to go back. They went back to their old haunts, they just couldn't stand it. They much preferred to live in Dockhead or some place like that, rather than live here, in Downham, in a semi-rural area.

John Edwin Smith (Downham)

I was thirteen when we moved from the East End of London down to Dagenham, which was really the country. In fact my mother said to me, "We're going to the country," and I was not delighted. I just couldn't settle once we moved. I was always going back to the East End once I started work at fourteen and had a bit of money. I was going back to all the old haunts and all my old friends and that carried on for years. I just couldn't tolerate Dagenham. There was nothing here. Nice and open, but I just couldn't stand it.

George Herbert (Becontree)

I missed the East End when I first came here. I didn't have my mum to help me and it was a terrible, terrible wrench. My eldest boy was about seven, oh, he cried his eyes out. Oh, I can see him now. He sat on the back step of the new house and said, "Oh take me back, take me back, don't let me stop here!"

My husband never stopped down here at first. He'd do his work, come home, have his tea and go back up to London. My mother still lived there and I used to go up too.

For about the first six months all I'd do everyday was get my shopping, and get my dinner, and then sit in the park. I wasn't happy but of course I had to get used to it. It took me about four months to settle down and my husband stopped going to London after a while.

Amelia Cogley (Becontree)

I remember we didn't feel that we fitted in with the community, people weren't friendly, not like today. We didn't really have neighbours because Mum had her own gateway. We had the school next door and there wasn't anybody near us, not like being under a porch, which is more neighbourly.

Daphne Maynard (Castelnau)

LIVING ON A BUILDING SITE

Almost everyone in the houses had moved, on our estate, during the summer holidays of 1934. We knew nobody, not a soul and the building of the estate went on all around us. During the day there was a great deal of noise, dust and activity. Nobody was happy because there was so much noise all the time. The builders had these big chain saws and diesel engines. They roared away all the time cutting down trees, digging up roots and gouging out holes all around us. Even though we kept the windows closed, the dust got inside the house and covered all the furniture, and all the women complained bitterly about their clean washing on the lines being covered with smuts.

When we went out we had to pick our way over rutted earth and piles of mud and, when it rained, everywhere was a sea of mud. It was impossible to go out without wellington boots, and we hadn't got any. And I remember the builders put down planks for us to walk on.

During this summer, my sister and I had almost unlimited freedom. We roamed the fields and lanes as we liked, provided we kept together. We had strict instructions not to talk to any of the workmen or to go into any house, finished or not, in case something terrible happened to us. What that 'something' was we were never told, but we didn't dare disobey Mum's instructions. That whole summer spent in the open air did wonders for my health and my parents were glad that they had moved out of London, even though it meant having to leave family and friends behind.

Dorothy Barton (St Helier)

GETTING INTO MISCHIEF

When we moved to the estate in 1922, Dover House Road was just gravel with two rows of sleepers laid over the top. Only one side of Elmshaw Road where we lived was built and opposite us was all this scaffolding.

On Saturdays when the builders were gone and all their stuff was left out in the open, we kids used to have a whale of a time and race around the estate. Where the foundations of the houses were laid, we used to be soldiers and play 'war' in them. We used to have brick fights and sword fights.

There used to be a watchman, a great big fat bloke and we called him 'Beer Barrel'. I remember there was a tarmac shelter and we used to throw pebbles and handfuls of rubble at him and then make him chase us. Of course he couldn't catch us, he was so fat. We would also climb all over the scaffolding. Then with our bows and arrows, we'd fire at poor old Beer Barrel.

Inside the houses were these fireplaces which had a built-in oven. The builders used to hide their tea and tins of condensed milk in them and we would pinch it and make our own tea. On each corner of a set of buildings, was a lake of limewash and the builders used to put a plank across this lake. Well we used to run across the lake. The last kid running over one day bounced up and down on the plank and of course fell into the lime. We took him home and his mother slung him into a bath of cold water, which was the worst thing she could have done. He came out like a Red Indian!

Workers erecting steel houses, Watling

There was a little railway, on a narrow gauge, that ran round the estate and up the Dover House Road. Bits and pieces like bricks and mortar were loaded onto these railway containers and carried round. We used to come down Dover House Road on this railway. Oh, it was great fun until a friend of ours fell off the railway as we were coming down Dover House Road. The wheel of the truck went wrong and she smashed up her arm.

Jim Evans (Roehampton)

BREAKING THE ICE

When we moved to Watling the quietness really disturbed my father because he was used to so much noise. But after a few months we all settled down to the quiet.

Mum didn't settle in so easily as the rest of the family. She was left at home, while Dad was out at work all day, and us children made new friends at school. She loved the outlook and the place but she missed her friends and was very depressed. You see my mother had no family, her mother having died before I was born, so she had to cope with the move on her own.

We'd been on the estate some six weeks before we discussed how we all felt about Burnt Oak, Watling. I remember Mother broke down and ran upstairs crying! Eventually she came back down to say she

was sorry. And my brother said, "Dad said would we like to stay or go back to Kings Cross? We want to stay here." She thought it was horrible of Dad to ask us, and said she would sooner leave as she was missing her friends.

It even got to the stage when Mother wouldn't eat and Dad thought of going back to Kings Cross. I remember when she saw us into bed, she wouldn't sit with Dad and listen to the wireless but go into her room and have a cry.

Father got us a travel pass and we went back to our old neighbourhood for a visit. Mother was in her element. But when we was coming home you could see a great difference in her.

Mother went to this Ladies coffee morning down at the Church Hall. She would come back and say, "Oh, I don't think I like it. The people are not like they were in Kings Cross. I don't like them as much." But she really didn't want to give it a chance, that was the bottom of it. My father had the worst deal of all because he liked it here.

She really didn't get settled until she got friendly with a neighbour who had a mentally handicapped daughter. He was all betwixt and between because his wife was about to go into hospital. Well, Mother offered to help and I remember she cleaned his house and got his evening meals ready. Eventually people came up and said to her, "Oh, that was nice

51

of you to help out," and all that sort of thing and it broke the ice for her. After that she got friendly with people and no way would she move out of Burnt Oak then.

When you came along the street you'd say, "How do you do?" and all that sort of thing. And I suppose it's because we all wore a scarf and cap, all the same class of people. Some may have earned a pound or two more than others but I don't think anybody thought much about that. They all realised they had little families to keep going and they knew that was a struggle.

May Millbank (Watling)

TOTTERS NEXT DOOR!

The house next door was empty when one day these people turned up with a horse and cart and a few bits of furniture. A parcel had just been delivered to me and while my front door was open this little girl came and stood in front of me. She was wearing a dirty frock and had the dirtiest nose you ever saw. Standing beside her was a woman with a black frock, which was split, so that I could see her underclothes.

"I've come to live with you," the little girl said. "Oh have you, that's nice," I replied, and I thought, "Oh, my God what have we got here? We've got new people next door and they seem a bit funny."

That evening, we were having dinner in the sitting room, when Dad put down his knife and fork and said, "Do you know what we've got? We've got totters living next door!" "What are they?" I asked. "They're rag and bone people and they've come down from London, and they've moved next door."

Well, I soon got talking to them over the back and they hadn't got an idea of anything. They used to hang the washing over the line and it was as black as your hat. My neighbour, she would say to me, "How do you get your sheets white?" "Well I use bleach," I said, which I didn't, but after that her washing improved.

Then I supplied her with some curtains. It was for my own sake as well as hers, because it looked better as you came through the gate. Her little girl said to me, "How do you keep your doorstep clean Mrs Knight?" So I told them about red cardinal and gave her some. I gave them an awful lot of stuff one way and another for their benefit and they really tried to improve.

My neighbour really bucked up her ideas and dressed her kids nice and she would say to them, "Show Mrs Knight how nice you look." And these two girls used to stand there for me to see and I'd say, "You look very nice, now keep yourselves nice and clean. They're a credit to you, Mrs X." Then you'd see those girls at four o'clock and they would be filthy.

One day I asked the little girl where her mum was. "We've had to have the doctor in." she said. "Oh dear, what's the matter with her?" I asked. "I don't know." Well obviously she'd had a miscarriage, so I made her an egg custard and went in to see her.

I remember there was nothing on the stairs, they hadn't got to that stage yet. Upstairs the poor woman was lying in a single bed with hardly any bedclothes on. There was a sack on the floor, which was her mat and a chair on its side, with no back to it. She had a dressing chest with one of these yellowy bluey dishes which you get at fairs on the top, with a bit of fruit in. It was terrible.

I remember when they first moved in, people were horrified to think they were living there, but we got on very well and they were always grateful for what I did for them. I saw my old neighbour the other day and she looked so nice. Everybody's better off now than they've ever been. I'm better off and so is the whole estate. We've developed into a better class of people.

Elizabeth Knight (Watling)

HELP IN TIME OF TROUBLE

If you were in trouble you could always call on anybody. They'd help you when you'd got married, they'd help you give birth and, if you wanted somebody laid out, they'd come.

Vera Andrews (Downham)

Before my brother died he was in the hospital for about five days and during that time I went to a friend down the road. His mother gave me my meals and looked after me from morning to night.

There was a double tragedy in one week because three days after my brother died, the little Woodgate girl died. We were real friends with the Woodgates, they only lived five doors away from us. It was a bit of a blow to our avenue and people from up the road came round, and I think it brought us together.

Donald Breeze (Castelnau)

We were all the same class, so everyone helped each other. When I was about eight years old, my mother became very ill and it was my friend's fourteen year old sister that came to look after us, making our meals and taking them up to my mother in bed, doing the shopping and taking me to school which was a good three quarters of a mile away. This is how people answered calls for help. On the other hand my mother was always called to diagnose illness, bandaging cut knees, treating sores, getting a bleed from up a nose, and generally comforting anyone in distress. Doctors fees were high and to be avoided if possible. Diphtheria was rife, and my mother was on hand to persuade the parents to get a doctor in. Many children died from this terrible illness.

Joyce Milan (Page Estate, Eltham)

'HENDON AND FINCHLEY TIMES.'
11 NOVEMBER 1927

THE STRANGLEHOLD ON MILL HILL

Sir,

Isn't it about time that Mill Hill woke up and tried to save itself from being trampled to death. Already the raw, red tentacles of that housing octopus, the London County Council Watling Estate, are pushing their way through green meadows, devouring everything in their path. Helpless residents, apparently mesmerised, sit and do nothing. The value of residential property in the district has already gone down with a slump. Can you wonder? Roads from the estate are drawn straight into the quietude of Mill Hill and Edgware, and the LCC wooden bungalows face houses that sold a few years ago for over £2,000 This surely is a scandal. Have householders no remedy against such a ruinous action by the LCC. Though there is ample room, the smallest cheapest houses are placed cheek by jowl with better type brick houses. Thus the respectable mechanic has to live side by side with people from the slums. Why, too, build the estate so far from London? A man has to pay 23/6d a week rent and 6/-d train fare, and that's the LCC's idea of how to help the working man. Already 100 tenants have received notice to quit, mostly because the rent has not been paid.

House owners find they are having to move, but no one wants a house in the district now with hordes of ex-slum dwellers on the doorstep, and the threat of a greyhound track to add liveliness. Already there is a need for more police protection. People in Mill Hill have found their gardens ruined by children pulling up rose standards and stripping fruit trees. The language of some of them is such that even a workman on the estate told me last week that he blushed, "To think that such a female could use such a mouthful."

Another menace is that buses are to run from Mill Hill to Burnt Oak Station. This should be stopped at once by residents protesting. The London General Omnibus Company and the tubes have no right to depreciate the value of property in this way in order to swell their own dividends.

What is the future of lovely, how satirical now, Mill Hill? I suppose it will become like the rest of the LCC estate districts, as for instance, the flea bitten Ilford area. But all is not lost. Up Mill Hillians and defend your property!

Yours faithfully, ADSUM.

THE BATTLE OF VERDUN

The Barnes people thought they were going to have a lot of East Enders and slum clearance people moving onto the Castelnau Estate and they didn't want us here. There was this woman that got a petition up from along Lonsdale Road to stop us coming over. They tried very hard but they failed. They said it was like fighting the battle of Verdun, because Verdun Road, on the edge of the estate, runs off Lonsdale Road, so that lets you know the opposition that was put up and that was for starters.

The local shopkeepers treated us as though they didn't want our business. Now my mother was a woman that stood up for her rights, and fair was fair. Her money was as good as the next person's money. If she went into one of the shops, particularly the greengrocers, she was served badly. If she asked for the same thing as an upper class customer, who had gone before her, they would get what they wanted, but she was then served with an inferior product.

Mind you the community inside the estate was very good. You see, the whole point was, everybody had come fresh over to Castelnau. No two ways about it, it was a lovely place to be. Everyone was young and starting out together and they all helped each other. There really was a lovely atmosphere.

Mabel Wallis (Castelnau)

COAL IN THE BATH!

The people who lived in the more expensive houses just didn't want to know you. I liked the place but I just didn't like the people. I came from South London and I always find that South Londoners are different to the North London people. I'm not the only one who thought this but I'm talking about the people that lived on the estate, they all seemed a bit rougher.

The estate had an awful name to start with and it took years for it to die down. We'd hear people saying, "Oh yes, you're living on the estate where they put coal in their baths!"

Elizabeth Knight (Watling)

THE LEPER COLONY

It wasn't long after we'd moved to Mottingham that I found that the local people viewed us with suspicion and a certain amount of contempt for living on a council estate. People would say to me, "Oh, so you're from the estate?" as if you were from a leper colony.

There were a few social clubs and organisations in Chislehurst but young people from the estate were not encouraged to join and on the odd occasion actively discouraged.

I hadn't come across this attitude before because although we'd always been hard up, we'd been lucky enough to have been accepted for what we were, clean respectable and well behaved youngsters. So to be sneered at, merely because we lived in a bright new house, on a bright new estate, came as a shock to me. At the impressionable age of fifteen, I began to wonder if perhaps there was something to be ashamed of, living on a council estate. So for a time I told everyone who asked, that I lived just off Elmstead Lane, which was perfectly true but it also gave the impression that I lived in Chislehurst. Later on I realised how silly this was and I gave my proper address and any unpleasant remarks got the cutting answer they deserved!

Dorothy Barton (St Helier to Mottingham)

High standards of cleanliness on estates.
First mechanical road-sweeper, Dagenham UDC.
Becontree 1930

RIFFRAFF

If you were on the St Helier Estate, people with private houses thought you were riffraff.

Vi (St Helier)

The 'Downham Wall' built by private residents to distance themselves from council tenants.
General view from Alexandra Crescent, Bromley, 1927

WORK AND TRANSPORT

Baring Road Tram Terminus, Downham, May 1929

BUSES AND TRAMS

Our road was not yet finished when we first arrived in Downham. The tram stop, the last, was at the very top of the road and we were at the bottom. We had to walk half a mile along a cinder path to catch it.

As we became older, the road grew longer and where the trams used to terminate, a beautiful new school was opened. The tramlines were then extended by another half mile to Grove Park Station, and that was as far as they went. I can remember an adult fare to Victoria, on the 54 tram, was tuppence, and for the children, a penny.

The 136 bus which also travelled that route was slightly more expensive. Anyway it was more exciting swaying along and being thrown around on the top deck of the tram. We children always made for the rear curved seats, where we were thrown from one side of the seat to the other.

Buses could be hailed anywhere. Mum or Dad would just stop, raise their hand, and a big red monster would pull up and take us on board. It was tuppence to Bromley and half fare for children. Very few children ever travelled by public transport then, as walking was the order of the day.

Phyllis Rhoden (Downham)

PRIVATE BUSES

When we moved up here in 1922, people didn't want to come to Roehampton because there was no tube or bus route. Two private bus drivers lived on the estate and I remember seeing each of their buses parked outside their homes. One bus was called the 'Overland' and the other 'The White Rose'. There weren't many drivers then and there were no cars on the estate. A bus driver was a very good job and if you had a driving licence then it was something.

In those days it was all private buses along the Upper Richmond Road and we didn't get a bus route until the Doverhouse Road was finished. In those days the last bus, the number 30, was half past ten at night. If you went to a film or a show in the West End, you had to make your own way home. You either got a train to Barnes, or walked the two and a half miles from Hammersmith.

Jim Evans (Roehampton)

THE BUS DRIVER

My father was a bus driver and worked at Nunhead Garage when we moved to Downham. It was about a quarter of an hour's walk from where we used to live, but his moving to Downham was at great personal inconvenience because he was on early and late shifts. In those days you didn't have staff buses to take you into work and if you had to be on at four o'clock in the morning you didn't have the transport to get you there. It was your job to be at the garage and my father would have to walk a good hour or more.

George Evans (Downham)

TRAINS

To us that lived in Islington, Burnt Oak was right out in the country. My brother and his family were among the first to move onto the estate and as a child I used to come out to 'the country' at weekends to visit them. We got to Burnt Oak, on the Northern Line, from The Angel. There was one single underground line that used to finish at Edgware which was quite new. The trains were all nice and it was like a country line.

When the estate was being built, there was quite a bit of work as factories were starting to open up along the Northern Line, down the Edgware Road and in Colindale. The factories had come out to accommodate the people that lived here as the whole area was expanding.

Violet Bunyan (Watling)

A LONG WALK TO THE STATION

Father was lucky because he was a railwayman and had free travel. The nearest station was Chadwell Heath. Poor devil, it was about one and a half miles to the station. There was no way of getting there, so he had to walk one and a half miles to the station to get to work and one and a half miles to get home. It never changed in his time, he did the same old walk till he retired.

George Herbert (Becontree)

My husband was an electrician and worked in Ladbroke Grove W10. When we moved to Watling it meant he had further to travel. There were no buses in Watling so my husband would have to walk, rain or snow, about a mile to catch the train.

Elizabeth Knight (Watling)

LONDON COUNTY COUNCIL

BECONTREE ESTATE

(Population 115,000)

SITES FOR FACTORIES ARE AVAILABLE

HOUSES, CHURCHES, SCHOOLS, SHOPPING CENTRES, CINEMAS, etc.
have been provided

The Northern sections of the Estate can be reached by train from Liverpool Street and Fenchurch Street to Goodmayes and Chadwell Heath Stations, and the Southern sections by District and L.M.S. Railways to Upney, Becontree, Heathway and Dagenham Stations

Application for Factory Sites should be made to The Valuer, Valuation, Estates and Housing Department, The County Hall, Westminster Bridge, S.E.1

Page one

AN ADVENTURE

I enjoyed travelling on the train from Downham, it was an adventure and I used to love going to work. Because of the influx into the area of ten thousand people, the railway wasn't prepared. Very often you had to line up to get your ticket, and the trains were late. In those days people didn't have a lot of money, so you didn't buy monthly tickets, they were just out of the question. If you got to the station late in the morning, you sometimes missed your train. The trains had tiny, narrow carriages and were old. You had to push to get in.

Richard (Downham)

'TOT (TRAINS, OMNIBUSES AND TRAMS) STAFF MAGAZINE.' JULY 1928.

REBUILDING OF BURNT OAK STATION (WATLING)

This will be completed in August and a spacious and attractive station will be the result. The rebuilding was rendered necessary owing to the rapid growth of the traffic consequent upon the development of the Watling Estate. A population of 8,000 already reside there and eventually there are to be 4,000 houses with accommodation for 16,000 to 18,000 people. In January 1925, Burnt Oak Station handled 5,317 passengers. In January 1926 there were 6,898, and the following January 19,042.

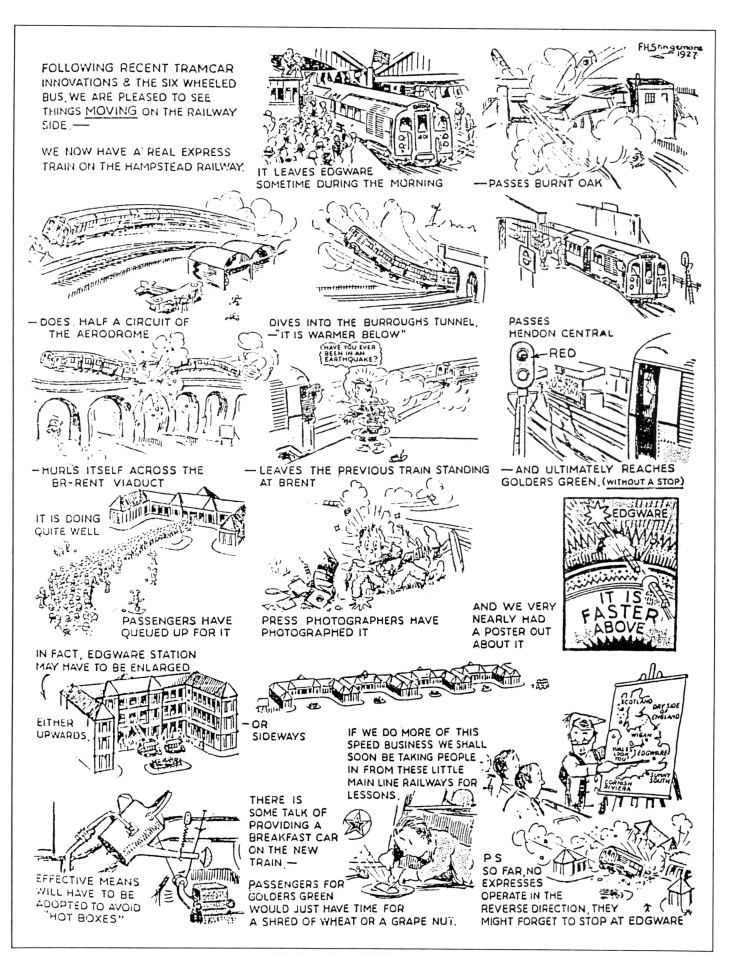

Cartoon from 'TOT' magazine

DON'T BE LATE

The last workmen's train from Grove Park, the nearest station to the Downham Estate, was a quarter to eight in the morning. You wouldn't dare go after that because the price would go up half as much again.

Arthur (Downham)

There wasn't much employment for men in Bellingham so everybody went off the estate for work. All the men would have to leave before a certain time in the morning to get their cheap train or tram ticket.

Patricia (Bellingham)

Dad was working in Hendon when we moved to Roehampton and he had a lot of fare to pay. There wasn't that sort of money to spare and my parents had to go quite tight on it.

Ivy Woollett (Roehampton)

BICYCLE

Soon after we moved to St Helier one of my father's brothers heard of a job going at the Surrey Docks in Deptford. Although it wasn't his kind of work, Dad jumped at it, having been out of work for well over a year.

Having spent everything moving out, we couldn't afford to go back to London so, rather than turn down the job, Dad managed to get hold of an old heavyweight black bike, the 'sit up and beg' kind, with no gears. He got it in working order, and cycled twenty miles every day from St Helier to Deptford and back, rain or shine, summer or winter. He would leave home at five in the morning and wouldn't return till six or seven at night. He would stop off at various people's houses and have a cup of tea and a rest. That way he was able to keep up on family and friends.

After about two years Dad stopped cycling. He had paid back all the money that his family had lent him and was now able to walk to Morden and take public transport into work. In 1937 Mum decided that the journey back and forth to the docks was wearing my father out so she applied for a transfer to the Downham Estate. The council decided to give her a place in the newly built Mottingham Estate instead.

Dorothy Barton (St Helier)

WORK

When the Watling estate was first built there was quite a bit of work as factories were starting to open up along the Northern Line and down the Edgware Road into Colindale. The area was expanding so the factories had come out to accommodate the people that were moving into the area. When I first came to Watling, I worked in a book binding factory but one of the biggest employers was the De Havilland Aircraft factory behind the Co-op.

Violet Bunyan (Watling)

There wasn't much employment for men in Bellingham so most men went off the estate for work. They would have to leave early in the morning to get their cheap ticket for either the train or the tram.

My husband was what they called the Labour Master in the docks. I used to get up at half past five to give him his tuck box and then see him off. He took the tram to Greenwich Church and then he would walk through the tunnel to the Isle of Dogs to be there in time to call the men and be organised by seven o'clock. His job was to call out the names of those men that he wanted. Those that hadn't been called would go running as fast as they could to the next door dock. If they couldn't get the work then they had no money. That is what some people call the good old days!

Patricia (Bellingham)

DOWN-AND-OUT-HAM

My Father was a wood-block parquet floor layer and all his jobs came by post. His firm would send a letter with the details of his next job and Dad would go from home to the job. When we came out to Downham all the roads were unmade and it took a while for the post to get organised. There was only one post a day and because of this Dad lost lots of work. By the time he got the letters, his firm had already sent for somebody else because he hadn't turned up.

The rent was always paid on time but if Dad didn't work he didn't get paid. Before we moved he'd had quite a good bank balance and the idea of eventually buying his own house, but because he lost the work, all his savings went. Once the post got organised, then the depression came. My father would swear his luck had changed by coming to the estate and he always called it 'Down-and-out-ham'.

Doris Pinion (Downham)

THE DEPRESSION

The General Strike was in 1926 and we were moved to Downham in 1927. It was the height of the Depression and unemployment was epidemic in those days. My father was a soldier with a very, very good career in the army but he left because my mother was so unhappy on her own. He became unemployed and had to tramp and tramp all over the place looking for a job.

There was real tension in our home because a man who can't find work can be destroyed by unemployment. Then there was my mother who was definitely overworked and miscarrying every year regular as clockwork.

May Day Labour celebrations, Becontree 1937

The rent of our three bedroomed house was fifteen shillings and elevenpence a week and I would have to go and pay it every week at the rent office. There was a Means Test and if you had a piano or any furniture, you had to sell it before you could get any money.

The conditions at that time, for lots of people, were dreadful even in Downham. There was hunger and real want and I knew of families who used to rip the doors off their frames and burn them to keep warm in the winter. There was many a time I would have to go over to the shops with a docket from the Relieving Officer. It was shameful and I felt degraded by the poverty.

In those days poverty among poverty stricken people was a sight to behold. When we used to walk back to Deptford to call on family and friends, we would see children in Greenwich that were poorer than us, who had no shoes or socks on their feet.

Eventually my father was able to get a job as a labourer working on building sites and he helped to build the Downham Tavern. My mother also worked and she used to go office cleaning morning and night. She also took in other people's washing and looked after their children. In one aspect my childhood memories of coming to Downham were charming because it was magic there, but then there was the other side, which was a feeling of real, real deprivation.

Rosina Evans (Downham)

The vast majority who lived on the Downham estate did casual work but I was lucky as my father was a bus driver, which in those days was a very good job. The man who lived next door to us was a docker and had very, very irregular work. His family had nothing as he could go for weeks or months at a time with no work, and in those days if you didn't work you didn't get anything, you was skint.

The man next door was very proud and I don't know how they existed. Come the wintertime, when you had the Means Test, he wouldn't go. I can well remember when my mother did the shopping, she would get a carrier bag and fill it up with groceries and leave it on the neighbours' porch. They would have known who it was from but people were proud then and the last thing you did was to let them know you had given it. We weren't more friendly with them because of this, we were just neighbours. People used to do that sort of thing. It was just a fact, a feeling more of the times.

George Evans (Downham)

FORDS OF DAGENHAM

Fords moved from Manchester to Dagenham in 1932 because of the increase in production and the better facilities offered by the area. The new site had a jetty on the River Thames so that boats were able to unload the London garbage, which was used to fuel the power plant. They also brought in the iron ore and took the finished cars, trucks and tractors off for export.

The plant itself was about the size of approximately nine or ten football pitches, with long oblong bays split up into sections. Each section dealt with a different part of the car. Monorails linked all the sections and these picked up the parts and took them to the assembly building. In those day nearly everything was made at the plant and it was quite a major concern, but the car bodies were made at another plant and the only thing that Fords bought in from outside were the tyres, windscreens, and the electrics.

A lot of the workers from Manchester moved with Fords but it also offered employment for people living in the Dagenham area. Working at Fords was the best paid job available but it was very difficult and competitive getting in. An unskilled man working at Fords, on a forty hour week, got paid £3 10s but a qualified tradesman who didn't work for the company, was at least £1 10s under that rate and he probably had to do more hours.

My father came to live in Dagenham in 1932 after having left the armed forces. When he heard that there were jobs going at Fords he applied. He went to see personnel and they took him on. I suppose it was because he had the gift of the gab and was also very healthy.

He was employed to unload the iron ore from the boats. There were twelve hour shifts and it was very hard and dirty work. He stuck it out though and eventually ended up as a clerk to a Personnel Manager.

I joined Fords in 1936 and there were about 10,000 people working for them. I was very lucky because my father had helped me to get a permanent job there which I wouldn't have got without that connection as it wasn't easy to find work in those days. I remember Fords used to advertise when they needed more men for the seasonal work, and if you were unemployed you went to the labour exchange and they would give you a green card, which got you an interview with Personnel.

After the interview you had a medical and if you passed that you were in. You were then told where you had to report to work, which could either be in the rolling mill, the foundry, the assembly, the machine shop or packing shop. It all depended how your face fitted.

Once I was in Fords I had nothing to do with my dad. You were in your own job and you stayed on it. I remember we had to wear a badge with our own number and if you were caught wandering about outside your department you were suspended or sacked. You had to look after your job. As to the seasonal workers, when they were finished Fords would lay so many of them off and it was unusual for them to be taken back on when Fords re-advertised.

Ted Knightley (Becontree)

I applied in 1929 to get a London County Council house on the Downham estate, but the council sent me to Dagenham and said it was Becontree or nothing else. At that time, I was working in the docks on the Isle of Dogs and had to start at eight in the morning. When we moved to Dagenham, the train wasn't properly in service so I also had to take a bus, which was often delayed and unreliable. In those days you couldn't be late to work, what with three million unemployed and no work available anywhere, so I ended up by cycling the fourteen mile round trip to and from work. I had to get up at 5 o'clock in the morning everyday and I didn't finish work until 9 o'clock at night, so it was quite an ordeal.

Lots of people travelled to work along the A13 and in the winter it was bitter cold. I remember when a lorry came along all the cyclists would crowd behind it, jockeying for a position, because it gave us protection from the wind. It was a dog eat dog situation.

I did the journey to the Isle of Dogs for five years. Then in 1935 I heard that Fords were looking for more labour. I didn't know anyone there, but I wrote in and got an interview. I really wanted to work at Fords because it was more money, less hours, and the most important thing to me, less travelling.

If you were fit you got a job at Fords and I suppose getting the job went on my physical well-being. It

also could have gone on my personality because I did build myself up a bit, adding in a few fairy stories.

I got paid £3 2s 6d a week, ninepence an hour more than in the docks. We became big moneyed people. In those days you would hear from the locals who weren't employed by Fords, "He works at Fords, he's got plenty of money, he has!" There was that element of jealousy.

Working at Fords gave me a good wage, shorter hours and good conditions. The life of me and my family improved tremendously because of the move to Becontree.

Bill Waghorn (Becontree)

UNIFORM TOWN

The chauffeurs and gardeners in Roehampton village were the ones who gave us the name 'Uniform Town' because we had bus drivers, policemen, tram drivers and postmen living on the estate. When we walked up into the village one of the locals would say, "Hello, here comes Uniform Town." It was all in good fun.

Leslie Charles Alder (Roehampton)

HEALTH AND EDUCATION

COUNTRY AIR WILL IMPROVE YOUR HEALTH

I knew no end of friends who were TB patients. Tuberculosis was very prevalent in those days and anyone with TB got priority points from the doctor to move on to the Dover House Estate. It was on high ground and had fresh air and open space, so it was more or less like the country.

Leslie Charles Alder (Roehampton)

Apparently there were quite a lot of people from all areas of London who came to live here because Dover House Road is on a hill and they reckoned, it being high up, there was plenty of fresh air. I got to know this girl on the estate, and she said, "One of my brothers had TB and we got priority treatment. That's how we came to live here."

Ivy Woollett (Roehampton)

THE DOCTOR

We had a lady doctor on the estate, Doctor Margaret Little and she was very good. She never charged much for a visit then. There wasn't a clinic on the estate, but a nurse used to come round, Mrs Perkins, a very nice lady. We used to pay the Watling Association for her. She would come round on her bike and I remember she was very tall and had the usual nurse's uniform of a black coat and hat.

Marjorie Rutty (Watling)

*Downham Health Centre.
Interior of Lecture Hall, 1932*

The main doctor was Dr Bee, he was like a community doctor and in my memory he looked a round jovial pleasant man. He always referred to you by your Christian name, always called my mother Harriet. Dr Bee would come at the drop of a hat and everybody loved him. I remember he wore a suit and waistcoat, and he had a little box of tricks. Dr Bee was always pleasant and never worried about money. If you couldn't pay, you couldn't pay, and he always did the best he could.

Vera Andrews (Downham)

Downham Health Centre. View looking east from Churchdown, 1932

MOTHERS AND BABIES

The doctor at the clinic for `Mothers and Babies' was wonderful. She was there for years and years. She was rather a thin lady with straight grey hair. Doctor was very down to earth and forthright and would tell you what she thought. I remember her practically insulting me at times and at other times praising me to the heavens!

When my son started to get onto his feet, he began to get a bit like his legs were going from under him, so I took him to the clinic. I remember Doctor always used to address the women she saw as `Mother' and on this occasion she made no exception. She said, "Dreadful, Mother!" I felt awful because I'd had no mother to ask for help about babies and it was my father who had always said to me, "Don't give him this, don't give him that!"

I can remember her saying to me, "You've got to give him cheese." And I went home and told my father, and he said, "You can't give a young child cheese, it will sit on his chest all night." But I was determined and I gave my son cheese. She also sent my son for sunlight treatment, two, three times a week at Lewisham Hospital. He was alright after a while and there's nothing wrong with his legs now, they are very sturdy.

I remember on one occasion taking my daughter to the clinic and the doctor said to me, "Mother, you must be a wonderful cook, because your child is absolutely perfect." I said, "Well my son doesn't think so." "Why not?" she said, and I replied, "Oh,

he finds fault with everything, but my daughter doesn't. She eats everything." After that I knew that I had done well with my second child even if I hadn't done so with the first.

Phyllis Rhoden (Downham)

ALL BOOKED UP

My wife was expecting Betty when we came to the estate so we were looking round for a hospital. The nearest one was in Epsom, which is about five miles away. With the influx of people, from this big estate, there were a lot of women pregnant. Epsom said to us, "We're sorry but we are all booked up, in fact you have to book up to get pregnant!"

There was only one thing left and that was to go to the council. I saw this man from the council and I said to him, "We've just come on the estate and my wife is expecting a baby in September." And he said, "I'll let you know if we've got anything." In August I still hadn't heard from him, so I went down to the council again. "My wife is expecting, I came down here in June to tell you." "Oh you'll have to make your own arrangements, I've got nothing for you," says the official. "I'm going to call an ambulance and you can take her to a hospital in bloody Edinburgh as far as I'm concerned," I said, and the man from the council says, "You can't do that." "Can't I? You bloody watch!" "Just one minute, try this address. She'll get a room of her own for three pound a week," and he gives me the name of this council maternity home.

When my wife was having her baby the nurse said to her, "You're the first patient we've had from the council. They're usually the councillors and officers with their wives that come in here." So that home had been reserved just for people from the council!

When we'd settled into our new home, one of the things I used to hate, I used to fear it, was coming home from work to hear my wife say, "Oh, by the way." As soon as she said that, I knew it meant a crisis and it was going to cost me! "By the way, Betty's ill." (Betty's my daughter) "It's going to cost us half a crown." So I would have to hand over my last half a crown. I would then have to walk instead of taking the tuppenny bus ride to and from the station to catch my train for a week until the next pay day.

Alfred Gates (St Helier)

She had a helper called Mrs Poultry and she lived across our road. Her hair was tied right back off her round face and she reminded me of a workhouse lady. She was very, very kind and did everything for about a shilling. She cooked the meals, looked after me, took care of my husband and my step daughter and I didn't have anything to worry about.

I remember she had the most peculiar ways. A few days after I had my son, I wanted to go downstairs with him. Mrs Poultry said, "No way must you take that child down in this world before he goes up!" She made me stand on a chair and hold him up, before I could go downstairs, and believe me, I think it worked because my son did extremely well.

Patricia (Bellingham)

Downham Health Centre. Interior of Female Waiting Room, 1932

THE MIDWIFE

A midwife lived on our estate. She was marvellous and everybody went to see her. I remember she wore big lace up shoes, had a black push bike and a big Gladstone bag.

After she delivered my son, and it came time to give her a present she said, "For every baby I deliver on this estate, a rose tree is planted in my garden." So we had to go and buy a rose tree. We watched her put it in her garden, which was beautiful because she was the only midwife round Bellingham.

A TRAGIC STORY

There were two retired nurses, sisters called the Glennisters. They bought the farmhouse, the only old building left on the Castelnau estate, and turned it into a nursing home. Quite a lot of mothers had their babies there.

Mabel Wallis (Castelnau)

The chubbier of the sisters was big and fat and more motherly than the other one, who was little, thin and very, very terse, very sharp. They were self-appointed midwives and had no certificates, which

63

you didn't need to have at that time anyway. They didn't have a doctor in attendance at the nursing home while I was there. I suppose they wanted to be independent of doctors.

I remember they had a young girl, definitely a maid of all work, and she never seemed to go out. She was no more than twenty and she used to worry me because it seemed as though her life was just one round of cooking, running up and down and cleaning. Whether she depended on those sisters for her keep, I don't know, but I never saw her smile.

The nursing home had quite a few rooms, the biggest one could take four people and when I was there I was in a room with three beds and I believe there were more rooms upstairs.

During my first pregnancy, I was under their care and I remember I went to them and said that my friend, who was also expecting at the same time as me, was twice as big, and I asked them why was I was so small. They said, there was nothing wrong with me, as I was a small person and it was a small baby. My friend also used to say to me, "That's the little foot sticking out," and I was worried because I didn't feel the same movement. I would say to the thin midwife, "Well, I don't get anything like that," and she'd say, "Oh you mothers with your first baby, you make such a fuss! When it's your fourth or your fifth, you won't be so keen to come over and see me." Then all she'd do is feel my pulse and my tummy and say it was just simply a small baby.

I was in King Street, Hammersmith, when the baby started to come. It was three weeks early and I had these terrible pains and was in an awful sweat, even though it was icy cold. I looked up and like an angel, there was my mother-in-law. I went to her and she said, "I must get you home." Well it wasn't worth taking the bus because the bus took too long to get round Hammersmith and over the bridge to Barnes, so we walked and I went straight to the nursing home.

I had the baby in this tiny room. It was absolutely bare, nothing but a bed, a table and a screen, which they never used, and lino on the floor. It was very sparse, a bit like something from Charles Dickens. My baby came and it was delivered. I still had my coat on. The chubby sister then whispered something and the thin sister simply said, "Oh the baby's dead, don't worry about that, just get on!" It was like she had stuck a knife in me, no feeling, you know what I mean?

My baby had in fact been dead for nearly a month and I was very lucky to get away with my life. Well of course they got in trouble over that. I stayed on at the home for about a fortnight and it wasn't run the way it should have been, not in a hygienic way. They only bathed and washed you once a day there, that was it. One woman said to me, "I'm absolutely smelling, I really need sorting out," and I believe her husband complained.

After the war in about 1946, a young girl from the estate had her baby in the nursing home. It was her first baby and everything was alright, then she suddenly had a haemorrhage and died before she got to the hospital. I think that was the beginning of the end for the Glennisters. It was then over for all midwives like them when the government brought out a law saying that midwives had to have a proper certificate.

Lilian Badger (Castelnau)

THE BIRTH CONTROL CLINIC

When we first moved to the Becontree in 1926, there wasn't a doctor on the estate. Doctor Bacchus lived in the village but you couldn't go to him because he charged too much. We did have a health clinic but it took three quarters of an hour to walk there from where I lived. Whenever I needed to go, I would have to arrange for my husband to stay at home and look after the children.

The clinic was a makeshift place with a corrugated iron roof and it was very, very primitive. You didn't need to make an appointment so you just turned up. There wasn't a consulting room and I remember they had this little enamel bowl, which was chipped, and we had to drop our clothes into that before we were examined. If you were an expectant mother, no advice was given to you at all and they would tell you, "Everything is alright." No one was there to tell you that you might have to see the doctor because something was wrong. Where I lived on the estate most women didn't bother going to the clinic but saw the local midwife and she would also tell expectant mothers that everything was alright. As time went on the council began to appoint qualified midwives and they made sure that there was one in every area of the estate. The gave them a house and allowed them to put up a brass plaque with their name on it.

There wasn't a birth control clinic on the estate and I lost an unwanted baby. The experience affected me very much. If I had known about an effective form of birth control, I would never have become pregnant. At that time I was quite actively involved with the Co-operative Women's Guild and was chairwoman of Grays Co-operative Education Committee. I attended one of our Guild meetings, where I heard a woman called Mrs Edmonds, a miner's wife, speak to us about family planning. After the talk I was asked to move a vote of thanks and I told her that I wished she had come a year before as I would never have become pregnant if I had known how to prevent it.

Mrs Edmonds was obviously affected by what I said as she asked me whether I had any objection about being sent to the birth control clinic in Walworth Road. I asked my husband first, because he was a Catholic, and he was very supportive of the idea. He said, "I don't want to see you go through the last experience again. If there's any decent way to stop another pregnancy I would like it."

So I attended a course which taught me all about birth control and I was fitted out with a cap. After that I was so thrilled, pleased and relieved that I wasn't going to have any more problems that I really went out speaking about birth control. I went and spoke to sixty women from the estate and I told them that since I started practising birth control I had never lived a happier non-worrying life. I then went on to help start up a birth control clinic on the Becontree estate.

In 1935 the council gave us a clinic in Becontree Avenue but we had to find the money for the doctor, the equipment and all the other odds and ends. I used to put up little notices about the clinic, and push leaflets through the doors of people who had a lot of children encouraging people to come and visit us.

Seven of us worked in the clinic and we used to charge a shilling a visit and the rest we had to cadge. I would go out to factories and talk to the wives of the manufacturers. I explained to them about what we were doing and then we would be sent donations. I remember I once came away with a cheque for a hundred pounds!

The clinic was very hard work but rewarding. It was eventually to set me on the course of local politics. You see, even though I hadn't had much of an education, I was a person who always wanted to know, "Why? Why haven't we got this or that, or why is it like the way it is?" Even though I was eventually to move off the Becontree estate, I still came back as I wanted to do as much as I could towards helping the community.

Annie Prendergast (Becontree)

A BRAND NEW SCHOOL

It was during the summer holidays of 1925 when we moved to Downham and there were quite a lot of new people arriving at the same time. I went to the Rangefield Road School on the estate. It had only just opened and the school had a great influx of pupils all at the same time.

The estate was big and we tended to stick with people in our area. The children who lived on what we called the Downderry side, the north side of the estate, they would have to go to Downderry School, so they didn't have to cross the Downham Way which was a very busy road.

John Edwin Smith (Downham)

Rangefield School, Downham, under construction

NO SCHOOL TODAY

I was six when we moved to Watling and there were no schools on the estate. I didn't go to one until I was nearly eight and then it was in these temporary huts because they were still building the Goldbeaters school. I watched that school being built and I remember we used to play in the trial pits which were dug before the builders put in the foundations.

My parents didn't really mind that there were no schools to start with because it was all open and there was plenty of space to play. You see they were delighted that they had come to a new house, a house of their own.

Mr Spicer (Watling)

When I came down here there were no schools available, they weren't open. So I finished school at thirteen and for about nine months I was just doing nothing, just going into the fields and pinching carrots and cabbages and all sorts.

George Herbert (Becontree)

LOST SCHOLARSHIPS

I sat for a scholarship for this school in Poplar, and I got it. I was due to go to this school but it never materialised because Mother moved us all to Dagenham. The school was now too far away from our new home and the only scholarship transfer I could get was for this school in Romford. Well in those days the buses never went from Dagenham to Romford so I lost my scholarship and I ended up going to the local estate school which had just been built.

Florence Essam (Becontree)

We moved to St Helier in the early part of the summer, so I didn't have to go to school, in fact there was no sign of a school anywhere nearby, so we spent all our time playing in the fields behind the houses. There was a wide deep stream in one of the fields and, together with the rest of the children in our road, we kept ourselves amused by building a bridge from all sorts of bits and pieces like logs, broken gates and fences, and anything else we could find.

After we had moved I found out that I had won a free scholarship to a fee paying school in London but had lost it by moving away. I'm afraid I made my parents' life hell for a long, long time over that and it took me a long time to settle down.

Dorothy Barton (St Helier)

THE RED BITS ARE OURS

The Lowther School was the only school in the district and I went there in 1932 just before my fifth birthday. The first teacher I had was Miss Fairclough for the junior class. She taught us reading. I was pretty fortunate because my mother had already taught me to read small words. All round the walls of our classroom were pictures. There was a cat, a dog, a rat, a mouse, whatever.

One of the first lessons we were given was about the Empire and we were taught to be very patriotic. I can remember as though it was yesterday, Miss Fairclough pulled down a damn great map of the world, and on it was all this red, which of course denoted the Empire. She told us, "That is ours, that belongs to us." That has always stuck in my mind.

Empire Day generated a hell of a lot of activity at school. All the little boys, who were in the Cubs would wear their uniform and the girls, in the Brownies, would do the same and there would be the odd party in the street.

School in Deptford 1930s

Dorothy Barley Infants' classroom, Becontree 1934

In those days every single person got a third of a pint of milk a day which used to be for nothing, and in the winter all the milk bottles were put on the radiators so that the milk wasn't cold when the kiddies came to drink it.

We had to wear a uniform of sorts. I can't remember what the girls wore, but the boys used to have to wear a black and white tie, grey trousers and a blue jacket with the school badge on it. The teachers at the Lowther School were very strict and I can remember the many times we were sent to stand outside Mr Mumford's study. You would probably end up with three or four strokes across the hand for being a naughty boy or girl. Nevertheless I remember having a tremendous pride for being at the Lowther School.

Ken Wills (Castelnau)

LOOKED DOWN ON

I came from a very good school in Westminster and when we moved to the Castelnau Estate I had to go to the 'Green School', Barnes Central. We were all made to feel inferior there. When it came to leaving, my mother had to go and see the Headmistress about different jobs for me. She said to my mother, "Oh, that's alright, she's only an estate girl, put her in service."

Mabel Wallis (Castelnau)

Interior of Junior Library, Becontree 1930s

67

A WONDERFUL SCHOOL

When we first moved to Downham, I went to this school at Lee. It was a rather old-fashioned school and I was there till they built Launcelot Road School on the estate.

I was one of the first pupils ever to set foot in Launcelot Road School and it was light, airy and wonderful. There were all these beautiful tiles on the wall and I'd never seen anything like that before. There were about six classrooms for the infants. Then, the boys school was downstairs and the girls school was upstairs. I remember we had beautiful polished floors. There was a big playground for us to play in as well as small gardens attached to the school.

Phyllis Rhoden (Downham)

classes. I think they were the children with TB and they used to have milk, and in the winter it was heated up for them. The open air classes were held in an open shed in the playground, which had windows covered with canvas.

Florrie Abel and Gladys Hanson (Bellingham)

A PROGRESSIVE SCHOOL

I went to Churchdown Senior Girls School, Bellingham. The boys were upstairs and the girls downstairs. We had open political debates, which were really very progressive and there were lots of 'out of school' activities for us to do. The teachers voluntarily organised clubs. We had a music appreciation class, and there was stamp collecting and the Brownies, all sorts of different clubs.

*Open-air class, Rangefield Road, Downham 1927. Mr Murray, class teacher on left,
Mr Hooley, Headmaster, on right*

OPEN AIR CLASSES

From five to fourteen years old, we went to Athelney Street School, which is still on the estate. The boys used to be at one end of the school and the girls the other with the primary school at the back. It was just an ordinary school, you didn't have lunch there, or even milk. The only time I had milk was when I sat for my scholarship. For the weak children, who had something wrong with them, there were open air

Before I left school at fourteen, in 1934, my class were taught how to write letters, apply for jobs and use a telephone. We used the school phone for that. Looking back on it we had a good education.

Winifred (Bellingham)

NINETY-NINE OUT OF A HUNDRED

School was reached by an indirect route since the railway arch at Westhorne Avenue had not been built. We walked about three miles there and back. My friend had a ride in a push chair in her earlier years, a wooden framed one with a carpet seat and back. We were both under eight years old and just two of many children attending the only school built at that time. It was Haimo Road, and it still looks the same after sixty-three years. We returned for the sixty years celebrations at the invitation of the head.

I remember the wild flower competition when all pupils in the junior school were asked to collect as many wild flowers as possible. These were put in paste jars on a long table and we were asked to identify them. My elder sister won with a mark of ninety-nine and I came second with seventy-eight. It would be very difficult to find ten wild flowers now in the roads around the school.

Irene Swanton (Page Estate, Eltham)

*Athelney Street School, Bellingham.
Dutch garden 1923*

SCHOOL UNIFORM

When there was anything like Empire Day, we had our photo taken at school. Kids in drill slips were obviously the ones put in front because they looked the best. Us that hadn't got them were at the back because we didn't make the photo look so good. The civil servants' kids had no problem getting drill slips but my mum couldn't afford to buy ones for my sister and me. I did manage to get a second hand one which belonged to the sister of someone in my class. My mum pressed the drill slip up, and the lady next door was a dressmaker and she altered it so it fitted me and was alright.

The convent in Roehampton Lane, where the moneyed people sent their kids, used to have jumble

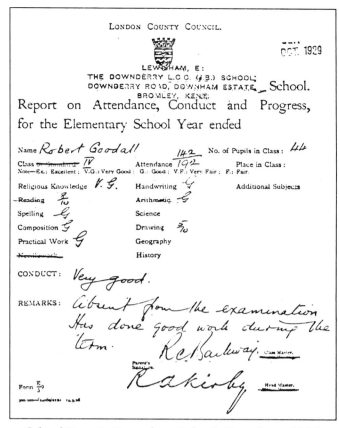

School Report, Downderry School, Downham 1929

sales every so often. Another neighbour, Mrs Glanville, went up there and she bought her girls, my sister and me a drill slip each. My drill slip was made of beautiful material. Braid and buttons were bought for us, so when we got to school, we wouldn't all look like convent girls. Nearly all the girls at Huntingfield had these slips, so it was important to try and disguise them in some way. Mrs Granville did us all up different and I had green braid and red buttons. And I felt a lot better going to school wearing my drill slip.

Ivy Woollett (Roehampton)

When I was at school I remember the teachers used to ask if any of the children from the private houses had any clothing they could bring in. Periodically they had wicker baskets full of clothing and the teacher would open it up and if she liked you, she'd pick out the best piece of clothing for you.

My brother got through to Hendon County High School which meant new uniforms and whatever. He didn't get a grant and my parents never knew why. Dad was only on the Underground, and my parents used to break everything down to the last penny. We knew people who had lots more money coming in that got grants. It was another struggle for my parents.

May Millbank (Watling)

Churchdown School, Bellingham. South frontage 1930

Churchdown School, Bellingham. Interior of Boys' Hall 1930

Lowther School, Stillingfleet Road, Castelnau 1929

NEW CAPS AND TIES

When we moved to Castelnau I was thirteen and only had one year at school to go, so I carried on at St Dunstans in Fulham. The people that lived next door had a boy the same age as me and we both used to walk together, over Hammersmith Bridge, to Fulham Palace Road. Half an hour it used to take us.

We did this for six months and then the council got onto the education people at Barnes, and said as we lived in Barnes we should be going to school there. So we had to leave St Dunstans and go to Barnes Central for the last six months. We had to have new caps and ties with all that extra cost just for the last six months!

Stanley Breeze (Castelnau)

THE ORANGE HILL SISSIES

I went to the Orange Hill Central Girls School which opened in 1931. It was a High School and I was the only one in our road who went there. All the teachers had caps and gowns and it was one of the finest and most modern buildings in London. It was built in the cloister style and there was a proper domestic science block and we had an art room, where we all used to sit around with easels, like proper artists.

I never experienced any snobbish attitude at school because we were all working class people. Those that did lord it over people, mum used to call the overnight rich, the ones that forget their backgrounds quickly. The people who didn't go to the school thought that we became toffee-nosed and we got the name the 'Orange Hill Sissies'.

I remember once we were told by a teacher not to mix with the elementary schools. I told my mother and she said, "Well you can get that idea out of your head as quick as you like because the elementary school kids are as good as you, so don't come home with your fancy ideas from Orange Hill."

Amy Ewell (Watling)

NIGHT SCHOOL

There was a night school at the Orange Hill School. It was very cheap, about half a crown for a lesson, or ten shillings if you enrolled for a whole course. Women mostly went along, though the odd lad would turn up to a class. I started at the night school when the children got bigger and I was able to leave them at home. There was a list of things you could do like cooking and carpentry. Or there was English, Geography and History but I was too scared to touch those subjects.

Elizabeth Knight (Watling)

SHOPPING

Trader with horse and cart selling groceries on Becontree

STREET TRADERS

As the estate was growing and quite a way from the shops, we decided we'd do a lot of trade, and at first there were no competitors. We were down in Barnes so we'd push the barrow up to the estate and spend the day up there, the governor and myself. His wife used to look after the shop.

Quite a lot people on the estate used paraffin because it was a cheap form of heating in those days. We used to go round with a big drum with a tap on a barrow as people didn't like carrying their heavy cans of paraffin up and down from the shops at the bottom of the estate. We used to measure it out for them. We sold it for elevenpence halfpenny a gallon. They'd give you the odd halfpenny. You know we didn't expect it, they were just appreciative at not having to carry it.

As well as the paraffin, we used to sell soap and soap powder and a big box of hardware. In the summer months we didn't sell much and we took mostly gardening stuff round. Lattice work, gardening

equipment, seeds, paper and paint, stuff like that. It was quite a job.

At first people weren't expecting you, but once you'd got known, then of course you didn't do too badly at all. We used to knock on the doors and they used to say whether they wanted anything or not. There was always somebody wanting something. Sometimes you'd get, "Would you like a cup of tea, I've just made one." We used to get all that. Being the first on the estate, the customers were very loyal to you. They wouldn't buy off anyone else unless they were right out of what they needed.

Bob Cubitt (Roehampton)

When we first moved to the Roehampton Estate there wasn't a lot of street traders, there were two greengrocers, from the same family. One used to do one side of the estate, and the other used to do our side. The only other street trader was a little fellow with an old Morris van and he used to bring round the groceries.

Jim Evans (Roehampton)

The milkman was at the bottom of the Dover House Road, and he was eventually taken over by the Express Dairy. When you moved in, in those days, the milkman used to come round and leave a couple of pints of milk. The baker came round the bottom of Dover House Road pulling a barrow.

The shops at the bottom of the estate were all popular and well used. I took up a Saturday job with the United Kingdom Tea Company. There was a chap there who used to go out in the mornings collecting orders with a horse and cart, a charabanc driver. He'd knock on all the doors, collecting orders from the customers. They'd be made up and we would deliver them in the afternoon.

Ivy Woollett (Roehampton)

man played the spoons to attract customers to the weekly auctioning of the unsold joints of meat.

A hot pie man, a muffin man and a shrimps and winkles vendor, all regular as could be, would come round. The Indian toffee man made the occasional appearance and a local chap would wheel round trays of sour toffee apples for a halfpenny each.

There were always gypsies coming to the door with their lucky heather and clothes pegs, which were made out of two hefty pieces of split shaped branches, joined with strips of tin. It was considered improvident to refuse them as it was said they would leave identifying marks for their friends. If we saw them coming we were conveniently out.

Ravenscar Road, Downham, looking east from Shroffold Road, 1928. Note Daren bread delivery van

Downham was visited by many travellers and door to door salesmen, and in those days no charge was made for deliveries. The most consistent were the baker's roundsmen, who came with a covered cart. Their counterparts, the milkmen, came from at least three different dairies, United, Co-op and Express. However, the most popular was Groom's, always called Groomsie, who with a horse drawn cart, could supply his customers with all manner of household necessities in the bread and grocery line. My mother being a keen Co-operator never patronized Grooms but preferred to visit our main Co-op store in Bromley.

The newspaper boy came round every evening calling out, "Star, News, and Standard." We didn't buy these as we had, The Daily Herald delivered, and on Sundays the Reynolds News. Saturdays we paid for the papers, and the insurance man from the Co-op would also come to collect his few pence.

On a Saturday evening quite a crowd would gather near the Downham Tavern, where there was an entertainment at Gorston's, the butchers. A young

A welcome visitor was Miss Jones, an educated lady, who took orders for dressmaking and knitting, which would be paid for in instalments of a shilling a week. Mother knitted all our vests and made the odd dress, so we didn't give Miss Jones an awful lot of custom.

Phyllis Rhoden (Downham)

STREET CALLS

We almost lived by dealing straight from the street traders until we got some shops near us. The milk cart was pushed by a man called Bennett right up the Dover House Road. He was a nice man and the children liked him and he did work hard pushing that cart up the hill. He would call, "Milko," and you'd take your jug out and get a half pint for a penny.

We could get fresh fish then. The fish lady, she used to come round with her barrow and then there was this firewood lady who called out, "Firewood." She had great pieces of wood, which she would cut the

72

Shopping Centre, Bromley Road, Downham, 1930

right length for your fire. They would help make your fire burn quickly. And then there was this other lady. If the kids took an empty jam jar out to her she would give them a windmill made of newspaper, which she had made herself.

The sweep used to come out, and call in the street, "Chimney for a shilling." He didn't live that far away and he cleaned everybody's chimneys on the estate. The sweep must have been a rich man with all his shillings.

I'm afraid we didn't always stick to the rule, to have your chimney swept once a year. I didn't like having the sweep around, oh, he made such a mess! There was no vacuum in those days so you covered up the house as best you could, but the soot used to get everywhere.

Lilian Beardsmore (Roehampton)

PLYING FOR TRADE

When we first moved to St Helier all the local shopkeepers from Rose Hill delivered small packs of their products to us, free, in the hope of getting our custom and this pleased Mum no end. The dairy sent us butter and tea and the baker, bread and cakes. Things were delivered in vans then, but my mother liked to go to the shops herself because she thought it was cheaper in the long run.

It was a long walk to Rose Hill where the nearest shops were. Mother did a bit of shopping during the week but quite often it was a family event and all of us went on a Saturday afternoon to help carry the bags home. It wasn't until later on there was a bus. It improved things quite considerably.

Shopping parade, Becontree, 1925

We moved from St Helier to Mottingham in 1937 and I remember, at first, there were no shops at all on the estate and we had to walk all the way to old Mottingham or Chislehurst for everything we needed. The only bus was a single deck one from Bromley to Eltham and of course by the time it got to us at Elmstead Lane it was always full up, so we mostly walked everywhere.

Dorothy Barton (St Helier to Mottingham)

When we first came on to the estate, we used to get the milkman, the baker and the greengrocer plying for trade. They tried to get your custom and it worked. How they plied you was, they'd give you a big box of groceries, or you'd get bread for a week. The United Dairy and the Co-op would give you a parcel and you had to make your choice. You could get practically everything off the milkman, butter, sugar and tea if you ran out, and the baker called everyday with his horse and cart.

We were pretty central living in Castelnau. Hammersmith wasn't that far and we did most of our shopping there. It was better then and had some extremely good markets. We didn't have cars in those days, we all had legs, and we were young enough to use them. We didn't feel cut off because the bus service was very good. You knew a bus was going to come along in a couple of minutes so that was alright. It was only a penny ride over the bridge but most people walked.

Mabel Wallis (Castelnau)

Shopping parade, Becontree, 1935

OLD SOAP AND GROCERIES

The estate shops at the bottom of Dover House Road were terribly expensive. Mother just couldn't afford to buy from them all the time. We had to run down the road for odds and ends but mostly Mum would go to Putney High Street, a couple of times a week, to do her shopping.

When my father was out of work I can remember we had these blasted relief tickets. During our school dinner breaks, Mum would send me and my brother to the bakers, which was down by Wandsworth Park. Before going Mum would say, "Wait till the shop's empty. Don't go in there when anybody's in there, and don't let anybody see you going in." Not that anyone knew us round there, but still. And we'd run all the way there to get the two loaves of bread.

I remember there used to be this chap with a motorbike outside the school and he would sell halfpenny sweets and toffees from his sidecar. He then went from his motorbike to a little van and started to sell soap and groceries. That became his name in the finish, "Have you seen old soap and groceries?" I never knew his proper name but he worked up a jolly good business on our estate.

Ivy Woollett (Roehampton)

2-20 Woodward Road, Becontree, from south-east

THE ERRAND BOY

When we first come to the Becontree Estate there were very few shops. There was a corner shop in Bennett's Castle Lane which was a good walk away, about a quarter of an hour. You could get most provisions there. We'd also go to a little undercover market place in Becontree Avenue. That had been there a long long time. It was a fair old walk, twenty minutes.

In the main, what used to happen was, you'd get a lot of vans bringing groceries to your door. They used to come round the streets with carts or motors, selling saveloys and peas pudding. They'd shout out or ring a bell, and we used to run out and get our stuff. We used to get so many of them. We also got a lot of costermongers with barrows, oranges or apples, that's all they'd sell.

Shops being erected at Green Lane North, St Helier 1931

Eventually when they did get the shops, it was at Five Elms which was made into a fair sized parade, there must have been about twenty shops. You had everything, fish shops, wet and fried, plenty of butchers and about three grocers. There was a Co-op which was, in those days, more or less selling everything. They used to call it an emporium. The Co-op used to be a very busy shop.

Jobs were very hard to get in 1926 but I got one on the estate at the Co-op as an errand boy, and I loved the job. I said to myself, "I reckon I'm going to be the best delivery boy ever, there's nobody going to take this job away." That was my attitude.

A lot of people used to have their groceries delivered in them days, mainly because the shops were so far away. It was generally recognised that a lot of people had their orders done with the Co-op. We used to parcel them up and I'd deliver them. First I had a trade bike and I'd pile the parcels on. I used to cycle for miles and miles. I loved it. Eventually they got me a tricycle with a big box on the front. I used to pinch biscuits and cakes, help yourself sort of thing. I started on twelve shillings a week. My mother got all that except for about two shillings. That's all I got. That was the way things were in those days.

George Herbert (Becontree)

A RIDE FOR A JAM JAR

The corn merchant used to come along with his horse and cart and he used to call out, "Soap, soda, candles, matches, penny a lump salt." Penny a lump salt was a big solid piece of salt for cooking. You could also buy a piece of hearth stone and that is what you did your step and copper with.

Every Sunday morning the muffin man came round. He used to wear about three or four caps and have this big tray of muffins balanced on his head, covered up with a sack. He'd ring a bell as he went along and just call out, "Muffins."

There was a man used to come round with a horse and cart. He had a little roundabout on it, that sat about four children. You went inside for an old pair of shoes, or two or three jam jars, something like that and you gave it to the man in exchange for a ride on the roundabout. He'd turn the big handle, which went round on a cog and the children of about four or five would get a ride.

My mother couldn't afford to buy jam in jars so she used to send us to the corner shop for a two pennyworth of jam. It was spooned into a piece of greaseproof paper, and you carried it home like that. You would get into trouble if you licked any of it on the way home. So my mother didn't have many jam jars, except at Christmas time, and then we got our ride. After the war you didn't see the roundabouts or that sort of thing anymore. It's a shame, it used to be lovely.

Lilian Badger (Castelnau)

We had regular traders, The Walls Ice Cream man, Eldorado & Noaks and 'Old Joe' who bought his ice cream on a sidecar with a motorbike. Indian Toffee, a substance just like candy floss but green not pink, was carried by an Asian man in a square zinc canister held by straps around his neck. He made a cone with newspaper, put his hand inside the can and stuck a lump of 'toffee' in the paper. It cost a halfpenny. Sweets were brought round by an old man with a pram which he pushed down every street. And then there was the roundabout on the back of a van pulled by a horse, we could have a ride for a halfpenny or a jam jar. This was worth a halfpenny if returned to a shop so was taken as payment. The driver used to push the roundabout with his hand.

Joyce Milan (Page Estate, Eltham)

A LONG WAY TO THE SHOPS

When I first came to St Helier there were no shops except a newsagent, a pub, a butchers and a greengrocers so we used to have to go into Sutton, three and a half miles away.

Vi (St Helier)

THE MARKET

We used to have the stalls up the Watling Avenue. There was no traffic up there then and when you did see a car everybody would talk. "Did you see that car?" Down the Watling Avenue there were meat and veg stalls. Mum went down there with the money at about six, just as the stalls were packing up and she'd get stuff cheap. You knew the ones that hadn't got a lot because they'd be out shopping last thing Saturday night.

May Millbank (Watling)

I'd get thirty shillings a week, off my husband, to keep house on. That was good money as some people didn't even get a pound. I'd go down to the shops in Green Lane which were better then. We could get fresh meat and vegetables and butter. I used to be able to buy a pound of steak and kidney for one and eightpence and I'd make a great big meat pudding or pie with it.

There was a man who lived near me and he worked in the meat market. Now don't ask me how he got the meat because I ain't going to tell you. I'd give him two bob and he used to bring me home a whole English liver and sweetbreads.

As we didn't have fridges, meat was kept in the coldest place. A lot of people made a big hole in the garden. You'd line the hole, put the meat in a tin, and cover it up in the hole. And it would keep Romford Market, was held on Wednesdays and you'd get all the animals there. You'd see the farmers, with their pigs and cows, and all that. I'd take the kids and sometimes we'd walk there and it would take us a good hour. Apart from that we used to go on the number 86 bus which left from Chadwell Heath and cost a penny.

It was really cheap there. When you bought bananas you didn't buy two, the stall keeper would hold up a whole hand of bananas and you bought it. There was one fellah who had a big sweet stall. You used to be able to buy mis-shapes of chocolate and tins of biscuits, which they called 'broken biscuits'. When I say they were good, they were very good! It was a day out for us, Romford, and it was beautiful, what with all the animals, but that's all done away with now.

Martha Wall (Becontree)

PRINCE MONOLULU

A three minute walk away from our house was Grove Park railway station and a few local shops. There was Nunn and Loat, the baker and tea shop, where you could buy a pennyworth of quite edible stale cakes. We very rarely got these as mum made her own cakes. The Grannies Dowden, two old ladies, ran the sweet shop. I don't think they liked children as they were made very unwelcome. Next to Dowdens was the drapery, Vincent and Radford, about the largest and most interesting shop there. The assistants were very helpful and courteous. I remember if half a dozen customers ever entered together it would become pretty crowded. The pure wools at threepence three farthings and tuppence three farthings per ounce were very popular. All manner of cotton ribbons, dress and furnishing materials, sheets, blouses, dresses and underwear could be obtained. Ladies could also buy their stays there, 'the unmentionables', which were displayed generously in one of the windows. I remember wondering why anyone should want to wear these peculiar articles.

Every Thursday Mother used to love going to the Bromley Market and going to Bromley was a weekly adventure. To take a return trip, on the train, from Grove Park to Bromley North, was cheaper than the bus, something to be considered, depending on whether Mother could afford to pay the fare. However we very often walked home from Bromley.

Market Square was a large rambling open place, crowded with folks from all the outlying areas of North Kent and the outer London suburbs. There were so many different stalls, drapery, clothing and sweets. The attraction to us children was the wonderful smell of paregoric lozenges (cough sweets) which pervaded the atmosphere so strongly that Mother never got away without buying an ounce or two. They were bright orange, long and oval. The flavour was as lovely as the smell, but it was impossible to suck more than a couple without incurring a sore tongue.

The gypsies would be there selling their heather and clothes pegs and we were always a little scared of them. They would say, "Lucky heather, buy some for good luck." The gypsy girls always had a baby tied to their backs by a shawl, so tightly, that the baby couldn't move.

I remember Prince Monolulu, the huge Zulu. He would yell out, "I've got a horse, I've got a horse!" Anyone that was interested, and willing to pay, would get the name of a horse that was going to win a race. He must have been about six foot six and stood above everyone else because he had this big feathered headdress on.

Prince Monolulu was a black man and that was interesting because there weren't any black people around Bromley. He was a well known figure and I think he went to all the markets. He was around for years and years and years.

The market eventually moved behind the station because they re-developed the market square. It was never quite the same after that.

Phyllis Rhoden (Downham)

THE CO-OP

Once the Watling Estate was built it became a thriving little market. People used to come from miles around to Burnt Oak. It was lovely on a Saturday with all the stalls down The Watling Avenue, and in the winter, they had Tilly lights on the stalls, big paraffin lamps.

People used to come from miles round to the beautiful fish stall run by the Wilkinson Brothers. They had the freshest fish you'd buy anywhere. There was also a haberdasher's stall where you'd buy cottons, buttons and button hooks. All the stalls were lovely but they have been banned now and a market has been opened up behind the station. Now you get cars parked along the Watling Avenue instead, which is a shame.

Co-op horse and cart in station coal yard, Chadwell Heath

At the top of the Watling there is a great building that used to be a lovely Co-op. It was built just after the estate and was one of the first big stores down here. The Co-op sold everything, carpet, furniture and clothes. On the top floor was all the offices and a restaurant with waitress service. You could see all over London, it was beautiful. When you'd finished your shopping, you could sit up there and have a lovely afternoon cup of tea.

There was another shop called Steeles, people could go there and pay off things, put sixpence down on an article. There was a card and people could pay three pence a week on it until they had enough for their pair of shoes or whatever they were buying. Steeles sold clothes and children's shoes, and at Christmas it would be toys. He was almost a benefactor, I know that he made money out of it but people couldn't really afford to pay out straight away.

Violet Bunyan (Watling)

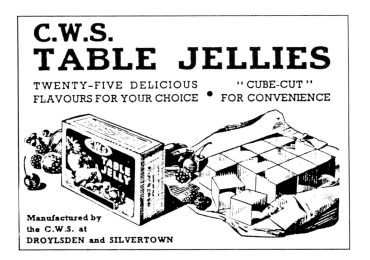

We would wait until Saturday night to go down to Wests, the butcher, in Catford where he auctioned all the meat. He'd hold up a piece of beef, give it a price and if you didn't say yes, he'd then pile sausages on the beef as well. We always had a cooked supper because we got our meat from down there.

We did most of our shopping at the South Suburban Co-op where we had Co-op cheques and you got a dividend of a shilling in the pound. The Co-op cheques were like imitation money. There was this number you had to quote with every purchase that you made and if you were in dire need, you could get a mutual loan or provident cheque from them.

Patricia (Bellingham)

OUR FIRST FRIDGE

I remember one day Mr Hibbert going out shopping and I said, "Bring me back a number eight battery will you?" And he came back with a fridge!

Mrs Hibbert (Roehampton)

Yes, that was our first fridge. It was from the electrical shop down the road. It was very, very hot and we hadn't a fridge. I saw this tiny little fridge in there, bought it and they delivered it the same day.

Mr Hibbert (Roehampton)

THE TALLYMAN

Regular callers were the 'tallymen' who did a good trade. It was a temptation for mothers to get clothes for their children, which they often could not afford to pay for, causing a great deal of hardship and persistent bullying and threatening by the tallyman. It was a con trick, he would leave a pair of boots at the door and then call back later for the payment, saying that once taken in they had to be paid for. This happened at my house, but my mother threw the boots at the man as he went out of the gate. We didn't see him again, but some women were quite scared, and petrified their husbands would find out that they owed money.

Trips to the pawnshop were a regular feature. Every Monday parcels of blankets and clothes being taken for a few shillings, and much prized diamond rings and wedding rings being lost forever because the money was not forthcoming to redeem them. My mother pawned both engagement and wedding ring, she bought a sixpenny ring from Woolwich so Dad would not know. She lost the diamond and ruby ring to the pawnbroker but luckily Dad found out about the wedding ring and saved to get it back for her.

Joyce Milan (Page Estate, Eltham)

I went pea picking once at Fowlers Farm over at Hainault. I had no money so I said to the family, "Let's go on the bus and go pea picking, earn a bit of money and save getting into debt." We got five shillings for the couple of bags we picked, then we came home and got our food.

I remember the tradesmen, they used to come around. They'd pester you but I wouldn't get into debt. One day a man come knocking at the door and he had some lovely curtains with roses on. So he said, "Want any curtains?" and I said, "Yes," and he said, "Two shillings down, and two shillings a week." I said, "Well, dear, I'll have it for two shillings but I don't know when you'll next get your two shillings." So with that, off he walked. That got rid of him!

Amelia Cogley (Becontree)

LEISURE

'THE TIMES', 4 MAY 1934

YOUNG WORKERS USE OF LEISURE HOURS IN LONDON. HELP AND FORESIGHT NEEDED

The lack of provision on the new LCC housing estates is surprising. A survey shows that in these areas the children and young persons of eighteen years and under number 104,000 - more than half the total population and that there are scarcely any facilities for juvenile recreation. There is an immediate need for ten or twelve centres with halls.

Downham: in addition to the boys club which Prince Arthur of Connaught will open, there is a branch of the YMCA, and a few church organizations exist, but collectively they can accommodate only a small proportion of the juvenile population.

At Becontree, where there are 65,000 children and young persons there is only one boys' club and girls' club with accommodation for 100 and a few units attached to religious bodies.

At Bellingham one church and one chapel do something for their own young people but only touch the fringe of the need.

At Watling the adult community centre has exclusive use of the hall. To this general survey must be added that the Boy Scouts and the Girl Guides have units which are cramped by the inadequacy of the meeting places.

How are halls and centres to be provided? The layout of those estates already developed did not take into account this need and there is not now in all cases available space for recreation, an omission which need not be repeated on the newer estates. There will be financial difficulties and it concerns not the LCC alone but the local authorities in whose areas these new estates are situated. This is how matters stand on the new estates, themselves the size of large towns.

NOTHING TO DO

When we grew up, when we were in our teens, there was absolutely nothing on our estate for us to do. No clubs, no nothing! St Margaret's Church eventually did have a girls friendly society and you could go round there once a week but it wasn't a club as such. Huntingfield School started evening classes and when I left there in 1928, I went and learned dressmaking. You know, it was a couple of nights out. The classes would finish at half past nine and if I wasn't at our gate by twenty to ten, my dad was waiting for me with, "Where have you been?"

When we were teenagers, it didn't occur to us then, to have a dance. Money wasn't that plentiful, even when I started work at fourteen, and I got nine and six a week, I had to give Mum some of it. Then I had to pay my fare and if I bought a pair of stockings that was my money gone.

The grown-ups on the other hand had their own club on the estate. Dad used to call it the 'Home wrecker' because husbands and wives used to go round there. It was more of a drinking club, where you got your drinks a bit cheaper. My dad never joined. I think he went up there once or twice but he got annoyed with the women who would try and cadge drinks. Dad was a pub man and he was well known as a drinker. He kept nearly all the pubs in the village going at different times. My dad could drink!

The estate club also had tennis courts. I remember one girl in particular, her mother used to play tennis. You'd see her going out when we came home from school at lunchtime. She'd be all dressed up in a tennis frock and little ankle socks and shoes. I used to think, "Why can't Mum go out like that?" I sort of envied that girl, because of her mother. It wasn't until years and years later that I wondered who cooked that girl's dinner. My mum was always at home, and ready for us.

Ivy Woollett (Roehampton)

THE IMPS VERSUS THE REDS

There weren't any facilities for children in those days. My mother was one of the leading lights of the Conservative Club and I was made to join the Junior Imperial League, the 'Imps'. We used to meet up at the Huntingfield School once a week. But we, as kids, found out that by joining the Red Club, the Labour Club, we could get more out of it. You got cakes and lemonade and all that sort of thing, more than what you got if you went to the Conservative Club. At the Labour Club there were a lot of women helpers and they used to organise games and all sorts of things. We would then finish up by singing the Red Flag.

Jim Evans (Roehampton)

A CAREFREE CHILDHOOD

Our new environment was in semi-rural surroundings, modern concrete all-electric houses built around spacious greens, which became our central playing ground. We had organized games, races and displays, all done by the dozens of children, there being many of them as it was a consideration to have several children to be entitled to a council house. We played on these greens until dusk gave way to evening, and then we collected around the lamp post on the corner. Our parents watched most of our play.

Sometimes we ventured further afield. Nearby was an old mansion house falling into decay. This we called 'The Haunted House' and ran all over the house like maniacs. The hallway had fallen in and the stairway was, by today's standards, hazardous. Yet we loved going there.

Everyone was quite poor during the late twenties and early thirties, many men were unemployed and most had large families. I often stayed with friends, and shared one bed with three sisters, sleeping head to toe. It was great fun causing roars of laughter with loud comments of, "Take your foot out of my mouth!"

Every Friday night we watched the firework display from the Crystal Palace, all the kids sitting on the green in the dark, and cries of, "Ooh!" and "Aah!" as we saw the display, having an uninterrupted view. We also saw, in the same way, the old Palace burn down.

A religious group came each week called 'Sunshine Corner' and we all stood around in a circle and sang 'I am H-A-P-P-Y' and 'The best book to read is the Bible'. We all looked forward to this meeting. We used to ride on the back of the Co-op delivery cart Saturday nights. When the horse stopped for groceries to be delivered, we all jumped on the back and rode to the next stop.

Parents hardly ever went socialising. There was a working men's club on the estate and some families went there Saturday and Sunday evenings where there were 'turns', a band and dancing. There was not one pub for quite a long way, most people could not afford to drink , and although poor they were hard working in the home. In all they were good parents, I cannot recall anyone neglecting their children, even though money was short and debts abounded. It was not 'the good life' but my memories of childhood are very happy.

Joyce Milan (Page Estate, Eltham)

Valence Park paddling pool, Becontree 1931

There were so many fields and open spaces available to play in. We could cross Westhorne Avenue as if it were a lane to reach a field that was a great playing area. It was lined on one side with a dirt road of huts, and their back gardens were ablaze with flowers. I can smell the roses even now, a real country fragrance. In this field was a large depression that was always full of water with people's rubbish floating about, old tins and tyres, but to us it was like a lake. Coming home from Sunday School my sister, some friends and I were pretending to throw our shoes in the water but at the last minute dropping them behind our backs. Of course I didn't let go of mine and it went sailing into the pond. What a dilemma! They were new shoes, a very rare thing, bought from Pontings at Easter. I retrieved the shoe, but my sister always held the incident over me and threatened to tell my mother if we didn't let her join us at play.

Summer holidays always seemed to be warm and dry. I remember taking some water to drink and a jam sandwich wrapped in newspaper, there was no foil in those days, and with sister and friends exploring Castle Woods or Eltham Park. They were only a mile or two away.

If we had run messages for the lady across the road, then we had earned a penny to pay for a swim at the open air pool in Eltham Park. If the day was hot and sunny then it was always full, and we had to queue for quite a while. I remember the smell of the creosote on the fence as we hopefully shuffled our way to the entrance of the pool. Inside the smell of the very heavily chlorinated water, the shrieks of delight from the lucky bathers, and scenes of the attendant skimming the leaves from around the edges, never fails to bring back with nostalgia the days of my carefree childhood.

Some days we visited the Tudor Barn at Well Hall which housed a family named Gardners. I think they could have been caretakers but we were never sure. There was a girl and her brothers. We played in the barn itself, and I can see the bales of straw now. We were also encouraged to ride on a very suspect boat like a punt around the moat and scrump apples from the orchard on the side that is now a bowling green and tennis courts. This area was out of bounds and so it was very scary to ten year olds. I know it would have been forbidden by my mother.

One day as we were scampering around the barn, my friend's mother urged us to hurry home as we had a new baby brother. She had just helped to deliver him.

When they started to build on the fields behind Kidbrooke Lane and the top of Westhorne Avenue, we still played, using the scaffold boards as a race track, running and jumping off at the end like a springboard. On one occasion I hit my forehead on a piece of scaffolding and came to grief on the grass, wailing and howling. My friend Joyce behind me was doing the same thing, and thinking she was mocking me, I got quite angry until I realised she had done exactly the same thing. Afterwards a man from the houses gave each of us a rose. On returning home, I related the story of how I'd bumped my head to my father, expecting sympathy, but got quite the reverse. His retort would be unprintable. Both my friend and I have laughed at the incident ever since.

Irene Swanton (Page Estate, Eltham)

MAGIC DAYS

What a wonderful childhood we children enjoyed, coming to a new estate with the country on our doorstep. Everyone said the air was like wine, that is why there was a T.B. hospital about a mile away. Every house had its supply of children and families came from all over London to this 'heaven on earth.'

I remember trudging up the hill of Burnt Ash Lane in the very cold winter of 1927. It was unforgettable in our first pair of wellingtons. There was thick snow and it was very exciting with the snow covered fields, on either side, for part of the way.

Opposite our road was a field and beyond that an orchard of apples and pears. I remember the hours a friend and I would climb a tree and sit reading our books, munching apples until we felt it was time to go home for tea. We had no watches but took a guess and I never remember being scolded for being late.

We had the most wonderful summers. During the haymaking, after they had just cut the hay, we would play amongst it and throw it around. I don't know what the farmer used to think when he saw his fields the next day.

Green Lane, St Helier, looking north, July 1926, showing preservation of trees

We walked for miles to find different woods and streams and there were loads of ponds around where we'd catch tadpoles and newts. There was a little tributary that led into the Ravensbourne, where we'd get our shoes and socks off and paddle. Unfortunately we couldn't swim, it wasn't deep enough. It ran clear through the fields on either side of our lane and provided a constant source of pleasure. We would jump and paddle and look for minnows, frog spawn, baby frogs, or flowers.

We used to climb the trees bordering the stream and jump off the branches to the other side. We children used to queue up to repeat the same exercise time and time again.

Just near the river was an orchard and there must have been a house there at one time because there were the remains of a door step. I remember we also found an old coin nearby, and we thought it was Roman.

Mr and Mrs Whitewell, John and Phyllis (Rhoden) on Martins Hill, Bromley, Kent, 1930

On either side of Burnt Ash Lane there were two little huts where you could buy tea. Workmen and travellers used to stop there. Inside each hut were benches and the workmen would sit round the room and drink their tea. I remember there was always a lovely smell in there. I think it was a combination of the tea being brewed and the fumes from the oil stoves.

These were the magic days of childhood which came to an end when my mother died and I had to take up my responsibilities.

Phyllis Rhoden (Downham)

Downham hop pickers

THE RIVER

It was lovely to be so close to the Thames and watch the tugs, the barges and the sailing boats go past. Most of the children were warned to stay away from the river, but I was fortunate because my parents knew I could swim, so I was allowed to go along there.

Along our patch of river there were several trees, which the boys and the girls used to climb. They all had nicknames like 'The Green Dab Tree', because someone had dabbed a streak of green paint on it. Then there was another tree called 'The Elephant', because there was a branch which used to come down, and it looked very much like an elephant's trunk. These were the children's nicknames though the adults probably thought we were completely mad.

Us kids used to beg, borrow or steal potatoes from our parents. We then used to go along the river, invariably to the same place, bury the potatoes, light a fire and then go swimming. We would be down there all day long, especially in the summer holidays.

In my age group there were about five of us who were good swimmers and we used to swim from the ferry steps, across the Thames and then climb up onto the Chiswick Mall side. We'd stop there a while and then we'd dive back in and come over to our roast potatoes.

Sometimes Mr Boswell, the old policeman, would come along and he'd say, "Are you children alright?" and we'd say, "Yes, we're O.K." He'd then remind us to put out the fire when we had finished.

I spent most of my summer by the Thames but there was one family called the O'Neills, five boys, one girl and Mum and Dad, who'd spend the whole of their summer holidays along the river.

There was another family, who will remain nameless, and they always used to go down to the river's edge and get driftwood. They'd pile it up, in the back garden, and everybody was horrified over that because instead of their garden being all nice and neat and tidy, it was full up with driftwood, which they used to burn on their fires.

Ken Wills (Castelnau)

TROUBLE WITH PADDY

On the other side of the road there were no houses and there was a field and a farm. There were apple trees along the wall there. An Irish farmer used to run the farm and if he caught you up those trees, he used to wait with his whip. You wouldn't come down off that tree until he'd gone. It was a thing of who would last out the longest, Paddy or you up the tree!

Jim Evans (Roehampton)

THE CYCLING CLUB

All my brothers were cyclists and I had a yen to get a bike of my own, so I saved up all my pennies and I bought myself a second hand bike. That, to me, was the start of a new life because cycling eventually got into my blood. I used to travel back and forwards to London, which was twenty miles a day, just going to work. I was fit and I enjoyed it.

Two children playing by the Silk Stream, Watling 1927

We used to belong to a club, the Eltham Paragon and we were about sixty strong. We had quite a lot of girls with us. There was quite a lot of social life within the club. We would go out at weekends and travel all over the place. There was a little racing group of about twenty blokes. We used to go racing, twenty-five, fifty miles, and go for runs all over England.

Richard (Downham)

FOOTBALL

There was an old boy who used to run the recreation ground called Charlie. He was a smashing old boy and was there for years. He used to keep the place very clean and I remember he used to tell the children not to drop their sweet papers and we generally did what he asked.

When I got older we used to play football on the grass. Now the story was that we weren't supposed to play on there. Why? God alone knows, but we used to play anyway. Round the outside of the grass was a cinder track and I can remember as a kiddie, in the course of an evening, running round that track about fifty or sixty times. Then, come dusk the recreation ground would close. After I got older I never went into the ground and I believe in the years that went by, the kids began to vandalize it. The council got rid of the keeper and there are no longer any tennis courts in use there either.

Ken Wills (Castelnau)

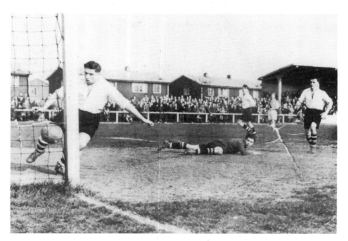

'The Daggers'. Dagenham Football Club 1930s

The Castelonians, our estate football team, used to play in the evenings over in the recreation ground. Oh, it was dreadful there when we first moved to the estate because it was all weeds and we'd have to try and cut some of them down before we could practice. I remember there used to be spikes sticking up out of the ground. They were dangerous but we still used to practice. We also used to go down to Barnes Common.

The Castelonians played Barnes Council. Some of their team were dustmen and those dustmen were big. They were huge. I suppose it was from lifting all those dustbins, they used to be made of metal then. So when the Castelonians ever played Barnes Council they would get roughed up!

The Castelonians didn't run for long. One chap got concussion because we used heavy leather footballs in those days. Anyway he headed the ball and poor devil, he died!

Stanley Breeze (Castelnau)

A RELIGIOUS COMMUNITY

My mother was a very strong churchgoer and the first thing she did, when we arrived in St Helier, was to find the nearest church. She enrolled all of us there, into the Sunday School, the Guides and the Brownies, everything she could think of.

We were not allowed to play in the streets on a Sunday but had to stay in and do something reasonably quiet, and naturally at ten and twelve years old we found that very boring and I went to church most of the day.

We'd go to the local church in the morning. Our vicar would talk to everybody and wouldn't just vanish after he had given the sermon. Then we came home for a midday meal. In the afternoon we used to go quite a long way to a Methodist Chapel, where we spent the afternoon in the junior class. On the way home, if we saw a Salvation Army band marching along, often with a portable harmonium, we'd join on at the end and follow them singing and dancing along with all the other kids. We'd arrive home at about five o'clock having had a thoroughly enjoyable day, because Sunday School and Church in those days were far happier and friendlier places than they are today.

There was a girls' club which I joined at the local church and we met one evening a week and sat sewing or knitting while someone read to us. I can remember Dad wasn't too keen for me to go there, as it was High Church and he was Chapel.

Mum enrolled Lily, my sister, and me into the Guides and the Brownies. We were still fairly poor and recovering from the time when my father had been out of work. As a complete Guide uniform was expensive the Guide Captain lent me a uniform which was kept for the use by poorer girls and it had to be handed back when you either left the Guides or had grown out of it. My mother was a marvellous laundress so by the time she had finished with the uniform it looked like new, much to everyone's surprise. Lily's borrowed Brownie uniform also got the same treatment.

We did a great deal with Guides in those days and spent many weekends pushing a lightweight trekking cart, borrowed from the Scouts, round the streets collecting jumble and then helping at the jumble sales, the proceeds going towards camping holidays.

The first time I went on a Guide camp, it was for a long weekend, and although it rained all the time, we spent the whole weekend running about barefoot, so as not to ruin our shoes and I had a marvellous time.

Dorothy Barton (on the left) with her brother and sister, outside their front door, St Helier 1930s

There really was quite a good social life in St Helier. It was interesting and the people were friendly.

It was quite different when we moved to the Mottingham Estate in 1937. My brother and sister went to Ravensworth Road school at the lower part of the estate and and thus made a lot of friends with children their own age quite quickly, but for people of my age, fifteen, there was nothing at all to do. It seems incredible to me now that these huge estates had been built with absolutely no thought for what people would do in their spare time. An enormous pub was built called the 'King and Queen' and it was supposed to be the social centre. Well it was for the boys. They had concerts and there was also a teenage boys' club. But for the girls there was little else save to join the Brownies and Guides in the surrounding churches.

Our nearest church was a tin hut so my sister and I went to St Andrews Church in Mottingham village.

We would go there every Sunday. I joined the Guides but none of the other girls came from the estate. I don't know whether I was older and at a more sensitive age, but I noticed there was a snobbish attitude towards me there. That was the only outside entertainment I got then. I did make friends with a girl who lived opposite. Sometimes we went out together either to the pictures or walking, otherwise there was nothing else for us to do. Anyway I used to spend a lot of my spare time, on my own, cycling all over Kent.

Dorothy Barton (St Helier and Mottingham)

We used to go round to the Congregational church, there was a good vicar then and they had everything going on there. Sport, dancing, Brownies and Guides, everybody used to go. From our bedroom window we could see the lawn at the back of the church. They used to have fairy lights and ballroom dancing there and we would look out and watch the people dancing on the lawn.

All the children went to the church but the parents didn't go. We went in the morning, and in the afternoon we went for a walk, always round the country. On Sundays we used to get the Salvation Army coming and all the children would go down to this green and sing 'H-A-P-P-Y'. Everybody would be singing or whistling. Now if you sing in the street people look at you as though you were mad.

Florrie Abel and Gladys Hanson (Bellingham)

I NEVER EVEN KNEW THE VICAR'S NAME

There wasn't much of a religious community when we came to the Roehampton Estate. Back in Pimlico, where we used to live, it was quite different. Although we were in town, our children went to Sunday School. The curate and his sisters used to call and you were like one big happy family. The children belonged to all sorts of things, Cubs and Guides and things like that, but we missed all that when we came to Roehampton because the church didn't seem to be interested. My eldest used to go back up to her Girl Guides in Pimlico and she really never got to know anybody round here. And our new vicar, I never even knew his name!

Mrs Hibbert (Roehampton)

THE SALVATION ARMY

There was a Salvation Army Citadel in Bromley Road, built especially for the estate in the mid twenties. The Salvation Army had meetings every week which were always jolly little affairs. They hoped to attract non-believers, or sinners as they were termed.

138 Oakridge Road, Downham. Vera Andrews with her family. Vera is front right

They had a band and I played the euphonium and sometimes the cornet. We used to practise about twice a week. People wanted to listen to us and they got used to seeing us around the estate and at Christmas time we used to play carols. If for some reason we didn't come round people wanted to know why, because it was part of their life then. I remember we used to play under the windows of people that were ill, tunes like 'Onward Christian Soldiers' and 'Under The Flag'. A lot of people think that the Salvation Army were miserable but they weren't, they were lively.

Arthur and Vera Andrews (Downham)

THE DOWNHAM TAVERN

There were quite a lot of things happening on the Downham Estate. At St Barnabas Church Hall they used to run what we called Saturday night hops. I can remember seeing a poster outside on the wall for a 'Flannel Dance', but being a young lad I couldn't understand what a Flannel Dance was because the only flannel I knew was what you washed yourself with. Of course they meant informal attire, such as grey flannel trousers and a sports jacket.

When I got into my teens I went to the large pub, The Downham Tavern. I wasn't fond of beer drinking but I was introduced to the Downham Tavern by going to the dances which they had in a hall. They had a small round box office and it cost sixpence to go into a dance and with the ticket you were allowed to buy a drink. There was an old chap, Mr Annetts, who used to run these dances. The band was up on a big stage and they played from eight to eleven o'clock. Old Time Dancing was on a Monday night and they played waltzes, Canadian barn dances, the London tango and other similar dances. On Tuesday it was modern dancing and it was the same price to get in but you didn't buy any drinks at the bar. There was a waiter and two waitresses who used to run around and serve you. Then on a Sunday night they'd have an entertainment. They'd put seats on the dance floor and have variety acts and turns on the stage. I didn't go to those very often.

John Edwin Smith (Downham)

DOWNHAM'S LARGEST "HOUSE."

HUGE TAVERN TO BE OPENED SHORTLY.

TWICE THE SIZE OF THE FELLOWSHIP INN.

It is hoped, in December, to open in Downham what is claimed to be the largest public house in the country. It is called the Downham Tavern and has been built by Messrs. Barclay, Perkins and Co., Ltd., the well-known firm of brewers. The tavern is more than twice the size of the Fellowship Inn at Bellingham, and has cost over £40,000.

Situated in Downham-way, in the centre of a rapidly developing portion of the estate, the building has frontages in Moorside-road and Capstone-road. It is of three storeys and has been designed on simple lines in free Georgian style. From a picture which appears elsewhere in this issue it will be seen that it is in harmony with the other buildings on the estate. The elevations are of Crowborough bricks with red dressings, and the roof is of red tiles. The frontage in Downham-way is 100 feet; that in Moorside-road and Capstone-road, 127 feet; and the rear wing 148 feet in length.

The Downham Tavern 1920s

The Fellowship Inn, Bellingham, 1925

The council built the Downham Tavern and there was something going on every evening. If it wasn't dancing it was wrestling. Parents with children could leave them in this little tea place next to the main building and then go into the concert hall, have a drink and see what was going on.

The hall inside the Tavern was big and there was waiter service. I remember there were these French doors which opened onto a beautiful rose garden. I used to feel like a film star at the Tavern as it really had atmosphere, it was lovely.

There were special concerts on a Saturday evening and I'd book tickets for my mother. For the children they had shows on a Saturday afternoon and at Christmas, pantomimes. Tommy Trinder was even in one.

During the war the Tavern was used for storing food and it has never gone back to what it used to be. It's a shame to see it now. There's a dumpy car park where the lovely Rose Garden used to be and I would love it to change back to what it used to be like.

Alice Ivison (Downham)

CLIQUEY

With the men coming from places like Bermondsey and Deptford they were used to having their local pub where they were known. Downham had the Tavern but it wasn't a local and some of the men missed the old company that pubs can give. The Downham Tavern was cliquey and you couldn't get to know people like you could in pubs so people got into forming groups. I've lived on Downham all my life and I wish there could have been half a dozen little pubs round the estate.

George Evans (Downham)

THE MARRIAGE BUREAU

When the hall was first built on the Castelnau Estate, it was used as a church. The altar was enclosed with big doors so it wasn't visible when there was a function going on. Then on a Sunday, they'd open these doors and it was just as if you were in church. A curate lived on the estate and he ran the hall.

Once everyone had settled down to living on the estate, a tenants association was started. The association used to run dances and for the older people they had whist drives. In about 1930 my mother started a social which she ran every week and it was immediately very popular. A proper band called the 'Two Bobs' heard about the socials and they spoke to my mother about playing. They came and played for us and were very good. After that we got another band which was four piece, drums, piano, clarinet and saxaphone and they were good too.

The socials were a shilling a dance and started at about eight o'clock. My mother used to make coffee, tea and cake and it would finish at about eleven. It didn't take long for it to whizz round that there was a good social where they'd got plenty of girls. Some of the Barnes boys weren't so happy to have the Hammersmith and Fulham boys come over and take their girlfriends away from them, but there was never any bother. Of course it was really like a marriage bureau for the children because the best part of us met our husbands and wives round there.

Mabel Wallis (Castelnau)

It went round the boys, "Oi, have you been over Barnes? There's a nice fourpenny hop you know." The boys would say to each other, "Have you got any girlfriends?" And someone would say, "Oh, I've got a nice bird over at Barnes." "Has she got a girlfriend?" "Yeah, I think so." And over you'd come and see. That's how it happened and the Hammersmith boys used to do very well!

Bert Wallis (Castelnau)

*Mr and Mrs Wallis' wedding cake,
Lowther School, Castelnau*

The church hall in Stillingfleet Road always had a little local dance on a Saturday night and of course there would be all the young girls and boys off the estate. Even the chaps in the band came off the estate and it used to be a very nice evening.

My eldest brother met his wife at one of them. She lived in Stillingfleet Road so it was one of the many estate marriages. It was really like a village because my husband and his three brothers also lived in Castelnau and they all married girls from the estate. When my husband and I were courting it was lovely because if you stood on our front door step you were hidden. At that time we had trellis over the front of our house and my dad had honeysuckle trained over it and the lady next door had clematis. It was just as well as there was a lamp post outside!

Lilian Badger (Castelnau)

A DAGENHAM GIRL PIPER

Soon after we moved to Becontree, in 1929, the Rev. J.W. Graves arrived on the scene. As there was no church a large marquee was erected in Osborne Square which was later replaced by Osborne Hall, the Congregational Church. Everyone was interested and the children, being curious, went round to see what was happening. There were all sorts of activities on offer. A boys' and girls' club, Guides, Brownies, Cubs and Scouts. Everybody joined whatever they could.

Mr Graves was very friendly and got on well with young people. He was always around and took an interest in the community. I don't know what made him decide to form a girls' pipe band but in 1930 he chose twelve girls from the Sunday School and without us knowing visited all our parents to ask their permission to form us into a pipe band. He told them it was going to be more than just another club and far more important. He said that it would probably involve a lot of travel and one day we would march in the Lord Mayor's show and down Broadway in New York!

*Pipe Major Peggy Iris of
The Dagenham Girl Pipers*

After Mr Graves had seen my parents they had a long chat with me and told me what was going on. I think they were probably sceptical but asked me whether I wanted to take part. We didn't even know what bagpipes looked like. I don't think I had ever seen them before. My first reaction was, that it was a bit ridiculous and only Scotsmen played bagpipes but then I thought it was something new to do and I jumped at the idea.

Mr Graves had a lot of faith in us as he mortgaged his insurance policies to buy all the equipment for the band. To begin with we were trained as pipers and were taught Scottish Country and Highland dancing. After a few months four more girls were brought in and trained as drummers, making us into a band of sixteen.

We had to do a lot of practice and it was very hard work but it was more interesting than the other activities in which we were involved. After about three months Mr Graves wanted us to concentrate on the band so he asked us to give up our other hobbies. The Dagenham Girl Pipers was to become my life and nothing outside concerned me very much. In those days young girls didn't have the opportunities they have now.

We used to play all over Britain at lots of church functions, fetes and carnivals, to raise money for different charities. We even helped to raise funds for our own church. In those days show business didn't have a very good name and people didn't think it was acceptable for young girls to appear on the stage in front of an audience. A lot of the congregation disapproved and they didn't think it was right that Mr Graves should encourage his Sunday School girls to go into show business. Although the congregation at Osborne Hall disapproved of us, they were still willing to allow us to do concerts to raise money for them.

Mr Graves believed what he was doing was right and because of the disapproval of the members, he left Osborne Hall. He didn't give up the ministry, he just resigned from that particular branch of the Congregational Church. He often preached there as a guest and at other places where we were appearing.

By 1933 the band was starting to get very popular. As we all came from working class homes, we were expected to get a job when we reached the school leaving age of fourteen, so Mr Graves decided that playing the pipes would be our profession. After we became professional, we weren't associated with any particular church. We were completely self-sufficient and independent. As we were practicing six hours a day we had to have a proper headquarters, so we rented the Drill Hall in Dagenham.

Any girl aged between eleven and twelve who lived in Dagenham could apply to join the band for a trial period of three months, after which she had to pass a test before being accepted full time. Eventually we had sixty to seventy members and we used to split up into four different groups.

I had always wanted to travel and it was my ambition to travel a hundred miles. When I left school our first engagement was in Exeter, Devon, so my ambition was very soon realised. I remember in 1934 we made our first plane trip. Admittedly it was only to the Isle of Wight but in those days to fly was absolutely fantastic. For most people who came from Dagenham it was undreamed of.

As a group we were very protected and were always very well looked after, even more so than the Dagenham Girl Pipers of today. We didn't think we were anything special but girls playing the pipes was rather unusual. Not many of us had close friends outside the band. When on tour we were not allowed to mix with other people very much and we had a chaperone and a manager. As soon as a show was over we would be herded into the coach and on our way. Spending so much time together and sharing so many experiences, friendships developed inside the band rather than outside.

Every year on the first Saturday in October, the anniversary of the founding of the band, we had a speech day, attended by the mayor and various councillors. After a display by the girls, speeches were made expressing appreciation in the words, "Of the fame the band has won throughout the world and of the honour they have brought to their native town."

My father's attitude about my being in the band was, if it was what I wanted to do, he didn't mind. He knew that we were very well looked after and there was never any question of us being allowed to run wild when we were away from home. My parents must have had a very difficult time then as my father was in and out of work and suffered from ill health, but I was never made aware of it. He never said a lot but he must have been very proud of me. He was unemployed when we made our first appearance at the Royal Albert Hall in 1933. We were taking part in a classical music concert. It wasn't the kind of thing my father enjoyed at all, but in spite of that, he bought a ticket and came to see us. My mother helped in a lot of ways too. She used to make our lace jabots and was very supportive.

If we hadn't gone to live in Dagenham, and if the pipers hadn't appeared on the scene, I would not have had such an interesting life. I would have probably ended up like the majority of the girls I went to school with, working in the local shops or factories, marrying quite young and having a family.

Peggy Iris (Becontree)

THE COMMUNITY CENTRE

We had quite a lot of community centres on the estate but our social life centred round the Sundridge Park Working Men's Club which was just to the East of the Downham Estate. Not all the families belonged to our club. Many of the men preferred to go out for their drinks at the 'Baring' which is still dispensing beer at Grove Park, SE9.

My mother used to go to a community centre on the estate at Valeswood Road where she belonged to the Co-operative Women's Guild, the Downham Tenants League, the Gramophone Society and the Women's Labour Party. She sometimes used to take me to meetings and I remember they were mostly political. No self-respecting inhabitant of Downham would support anything but the Labour Party then. The candidate of the time was worshipped and I remember the boys singing on the way to school, "Vote, vote, vote for Mr Wilmot, kick old Pownall out the door." That was Sir Assheton Pownall, the Conservative candidate, but in fact he was the successful one, to everybody's amazement.

DAGENHAM
BOYS' AND GIRLS' CLUB
ST. GEORGE'S ROAD

DAGENHAM, which has a population of 100,000, of whom, in 1932, 6400 were boys and girls between the ages of 14 and 17, has at last secured a building as a headquarters for Boys' and Girls' Club work.

The Trustees of the London Parochial Charities have provided the money to build the Club, and we now urgently appeal for help to maintain it. The Club members' fees and their own special efforts will probably realize about £40 a year, but the annual cost of running expenses will be heavy.

Besides the usual Clubs' activities, recreational work will be undertaken in the Clubs in connexion with music, drama, handicrafts, &c., and other purely educational classes will be run in co-operation with the Local Authority.

Capital is needed to develop the land at the back of the Club for a sports ground, to equip the libraries and camp, to provide gym. apparatus and material for the various handicraft groups.

An appeal is made to all those who are interested in the boys and girls of Dagenham to help them to help themselves. No sum of money will be too small in the way of subscriptions or donations, and you will have the satisfaction of knowing you have materially helped to fill a much-needed gap in the lives of the young citizens of Dagenham.

JANET LACEY,
Clubs Secretary.

Baring Road tram terminus, Downham 1929. Note 'Vote for Wilmot' slogan on car

The churches had their various activities such as the Boy's Brigade which was regularly heard parading the streets of Downham with their band. Of course we all knew the comic words of their signature tune:

> Here come the Boys Brigade,
> Covered in marmalade,
> A tuppenny ha'penny pill box,
> And half a yard of braid.

Phyllis Rhoden (Downham)

The Duchess of York opening Dagenham Boys and Girls Club, Mottingham

LOCAL BENEFACTOR SIR JOHN LAING

Sir John Laing, the builder, was concerned about the working class. He knew about the Watling estate, and thought, "Well that's an ideal area to evangelise, to get people to know the Lord." So he built the Woodcroft Hall.

When it was being built I remember my father saying, "I don't know what they are building on the corner there. I think it must be a bank, because the walls are so thick."

I remember the scaffolding, it wasn't metal like you get today but just old barrels with sand or soil in and timber upright poles. The scaffolding was put in the barrels and they were all tied together to make the scaffolding all round the building. It was boarded up so we couldn't get on it. There was this pile of sand and I would play with two or three lads, in the sand, with a couple of old tin soldiers. We used to dig out pockets in the sand with our hands, and put the soldiers in there.

Mr Spicer (Watling)

On Sunday I went to Woodcroft Hall of the Plymouth Brethren, which was built especially for the estate. Sir John Laing and Roland Webb were in charge of it and they used to run the services. Sir John Laing was a very nice man and I remember he was tall, with greyish hair and a roundish sort of face.

We wasn't made to go to church but were asked by my mother. I went to the breaking of the bread in the morning, bible classes in the afternoon and at half past six, evensong.

In the summer the people from the church used to go up to Sir John Laing's house in Mill Hill. That was our Bank Holiday treat. There were swings and see-saws there and they gave you something to eat like sandwiches and orange juice.

Marjorie Rutty (Watling)

There were no schools on the Watling Estate for quite some time after it opened in 1926 so it was decided that a Sunday School should be started at the Woodcroft Hall.

Mr Adams was the man responsible for the Sunday School and he was taken aback by the number of children who came to that first Sunday meeting. The response had been overwhelming. This was because most parents were only too glad of the opportunity to get rid of their kids for a couple of hours and know that they weren't in trouble. There also wasn't much competition then for organising children's activities.

Mr Adams quickly got some teachers in and within two or three weeks had got the Sunday School absolutely organised. He divided the hall underneath the church with curtains so that different classes could be held at the same time. He then expanded from the basement to the main hall. A hut was then built outside to cope with the large numbers of children and my father was very pleased with the response. As for the grown-ups, they came to the evening meetings. There were maybe three or four hundred of them and the Woodcroft Hall soon built up its members.

There used to be Sunday School treats for the children and they would go off to somewhere like Burnham Beeches which was really wild country then. Sometimes funny old buses were hired, but lorries from the firm did most of the trips with their wooden benches and canvas covers.

The children also came to my father's house in Mill Hill. Sometimes there were as many as three hundred of them in the garden. They also used the field in front of the garden which was lovely because it had a wood. My father had bought the field in the early 1930s, initially as protection from these terrible builders, but he also had the idea that he might one day build on it himself. He never did and it's still an open space.

Sir Maurice Laing

A VISIT BY THE PRINCE OF WALES

Back in 1929 we had nowhere to go on the Watling Estate. There were no pubs and the 'Green Man' and 'The Stag', the nearest, were right off the estate.

There was a Quaker called Cyril Harris and it was his idea to start somewhere on the estate where people could go and do things. The council said if we paid for it they would organise the building. So we had a brick collection to raise the money and it was a shilling a brick. We had to get so much money and a notice would be put up to say how far we had got.

The Watling Centre was opened in 1933 by the Prince of Wales. Once it was open the estate got better. All the young people met in the common room on Sunday afternoons. There were armchairs and a beautiful fire. Boxing, cycling and pigeon clubs were organised and there was also a painting class for the children.

Elizabeth Knight (Watling)

A community centre was built called the Watling Centre which the then Prince of Wales opened. It was a brick building, a sort of bungalow, and I thought it was wonderful. It's now very dilapidated. I remember the day it opened. There weren't big celebrations but we went to the centre and I thought it was wonderful to see the Prince of Wales.

Amy Ewell (Watling)

After the Prince of Wales had opened the centre, someone suggested that he might like to see a thousand people, a lot of them children, in this church hall so he said, "Oh, I want to go and see them." At that time the Prince was a very popular man. It was in the midst of the depression and he was very upset with the state of the country. He was very interested in trying to do what he could to relieve the poverty and visiting the Woodcroft Hall was typical of what he did.

Sir Maurice Laing

I remember sitting on the radiator at the back of the hall because it was so crowded. It was the boys and girls getting their prizes for attendance. If you got a full attendance for Sunday School you got a first prize. If you missed two or three weeks then you got a second or third prize. I remember the platform had trestle tables on it full of books. It was great to get a book in those days because we didn't get much at Christmas as we were poor and we had no money. Suddenly they played 'God save the King' on the piano and everyone stood up and the Prince of Wales came up on the platform and said a few words.

Mr Spicer (Watling)

Fancy dress party at end of World War Two. Morston Gardens, Mottingham

In 1933 I was over at the Woodcroft Hall where we were having our usual January party. I'd just been given a prize and was coming down the steps of the platform when a cheer went up. Well I was so embarrassed, I thought it was for me, but when I looked up, it was for the Prince of Wales.

The Prince was wearing a long frock coat with an astrakhan collar, long pinstriped trousers and he had a bowler. He was with Mr Stanley Baldwin, who was dressed more or less the same. The whole hall was full up so he couldn't have spoken to us all but he did come and shake hands with quite a few of us. I remember Mr Baldwin saying, "Time, your Majesty," and the Prince replying, "Be blowed with protocol, the children are enjoying themselves and I'm stopping here for a while!" That is something that has always stopped in my mind.

Marjorie Rutty (Watling)

Children in the countryside near the Downham Estate, 1930

CONCLUSION

There's no doubt about it but the people who moved to the Watling Estate changed and we saw it. Many of them had come from the slums where they had been living in appaling conditions. They were decent people who had never had a chance in life. Within ten years of them moving to Watling you could see the benefit especially in their kids who were growing up healthy and getting out into the country. They were going to better schools and getting the chance, if they were clever enough, to go to grammar schools. It was a great and tremendous improvement.

Sir Maurice Laing

When the estate houses were first built everyone was very proud and they looked after them. Maybe it was because we had a brand new house, and we did our utmost to keep it spick and span. As for today some of the houses are run down a bit. People aren't taking so much care of them with many of the front gardens being left unattended.

Peggy Iris (Becontree)

The Downham houses don't look like they used to. Many have become a real hotchpotch of styles. Some people have put in different windows or doors, used every style under the sun. A lot of people might say that the houses are plain but still I think that the estate was well planned and thought out and the architecture of Downham was really nice.

The problem about people who have been housed in a council estate is that if they had the money to get on, most of them wouldn't stay. I don't live in Downham any more but I have come to really envy the people who do because of their amenities and their community.

Phyllis Rhoden (Downham)

We all wanted to come to the Downham estate for various reasons. As our estate gradually widened with more people, we had to move with the times, meeting new people, making young friends, opening up various halls, Christian establishments and things like that. We gradually made our lives here and made the community what it is now.

The war really brought us together as we were all aiming towards one goal, survival. After the war people started to lose that. They were not reliant on each other and they became independent with some people growing richer and drifting apart from the estate.

Today you don't hear the good points about our communities. I and many others like myself are grateful for what was done and we have done our best to improve ourselves, improve the community and improve things for the younger people. For some it has been a long struggle and for others a pleasure.

Ron Chattington (Downham)

Downham Landgirls 1941

From cobbled streets, factory chimneys and railway engines belching smoke, the move to open spaces, gardens and a close-knit community of friends to play with, meant life for me in the thirties was 'just like the country'.

Irene Swanton (Page Estate, Eltham)

The London County Council Cottage Estates gave people the chance to pull themselves up, and the children from our estate school have all done extremely well. They have had the chance to become solicitors, doctors and bank managers. I think that all people should be given a chance, and I say good luck to anybody who takes that chance. I would recommend anyone to come and live on our estate as it is a very nice place to live, and I would like to see all families brought up in a little house with a garden like ours.

Mabel Wallis (Castelnau)

94

AGE EXCHANGE REMINISCENCE BOOKS

Age Exchange is a theatre and publishing company working with London pensioners on shows and books which record their life experience and their current concerns.

It is a feature of all these books that the contributions come from many pensioners, are lively and easy to read, conversational in style, and lavishly illustrated with photographs and line drawings of the time. All the stories are told in the original words, from transcribed tapes, or pensioners' written contributions. The following books are already available:

'On the River': Memories of a Working River. Recollections of older Londoners who have lived by and worked on the River Thames. Their stories recapture the sense of bustle and industry when the river was London's main thoroughfare and a crucial source of livelihood for thousands of families. The book contains over one hundred full page photographs of the river in its heyday. £15.95

'Fifty Years Ago': Memories of the 1930s: a collage of stories and photographs of day-to-day life around 1933. £2.95

'Of Whole Heart Cometh Hope': Centenary memories of the Co-operative Women's Guild, being the history of the Guild in photos, advertisements and, of course, stories supplied by older women who have had a lifelong involvement in the Co-operative movement. £2.95

'What did you do in the War, Mum?': This book of memories, photos and line drawings provides a clear picture of the wide range of jobs which opened up for women in the war years, and of their undoubted skills and ability in these new areas. These individual stories, full of detail and humour, project a positive image of women as flexible and resilient workers. £3.95

'All our Christmases': A book of Christmas memories by Greenwich pensioners. £2.95

'My First Job': Pensioners' memories of starting work in the 1920s and 30s. £2.95

'Can we Afford the Doctor?' was a frequent cry before the days of the NHS. This book examines health and social welfare in the early part of this century when people often had to rely on their own resources and remedies to cope with illness or disability. Childhood diseases, infectious diseases, accidents and more serious illnesses are recalled. Doctors and nurses remember their early years of service and conditions in homes and hospitals. The book has many photographs and illustrations. £3.95

'The Time of our Lives' is a compilation of memories of leisure time in the 1920s and 30s. Spare time stories reveal the energy and enterprise of young people who made their own entertainment in the days before television. Pensioners who are now in their seventies recall vividly the comedy of their courting days, the dance, cinema, rambling, cycling and outings of their youth. Generously illustrated with photographs and line drawings, this makes good reading for all ages. £3.95

'Goodnight Children Everywhere': A remarkable collection of first hand experiences of evacuation in the Second World War. The contributors speak honestly, in many cases for the first time, about the upheaval they went through as children, illustrating their stories with letters they wrote at the time and the photos of themselves which were taken to send home to their parents. Over 250 superb photographs. Hardback £15.95. Softback £9.95

'Many Happy Retirements': 'For anyone who has sat through conventional pre-retirement courses, being lectured at by experts, relief is at hand. Wisely used, the refreshing new source material in this lovely book from Age Exchange, with its case studies, transcripts and dramatised cameos, is guaranteed to revitalise even the dullest course.' Michael Pilch, Vice President, Pre-Retirement Association. £3.95

'Health Remedies and Health Recipes': Reflections by Caribbean elders on the subject of health and diet as remembered in Jamaica and experienced here in Britain. Illustrated with photographs, many donated by the contributors. £3.95

'Lifetimes': A sixty-eight page handbook and sixty Picture Cards, designed to stimulate older people to remember their own lives. The pack is intended for use by people working with the elderly. £20

Posters: Ten of the most evocative Lifetimes pictures are also published as A2 size posters. £10

'Good Morning Children': Memories and photographs of schooldays in the 1920s and 30s. £3.95

'Across the Irish Sea': London Irish pensioners remember their childhood in Ireland and their decision to 'cross the water'. They describe their experience of finding work and homes over here and reflect on their continuing relationship with Ireland. £4.95

'A Place to Stay': Memories of pensioners from many lands. Ethnic elders from the Caribbean, the Asian sub-continent, the Far East, Cyprus and Poland tell of their arrival in Britain and their experience of growing old here. The stories are told in English and in the mother tongues. £3.95

'When we were Young': A delightful anthology of photographs and memories of growing up in the West Country. A record of Age Exchange's South Somerset project in five villages, with reflections on the process from pensioners, staff and children, this book also provides a useful working model for other reminiscence projects. £3.95

'A Practical Guide to Reminiscence': A straightforward handbook for people starting, or engaged in, reminiscence work in day centres, hospitals, homes and adult education. £1.50

There are special prices for OAPs who wish to order any or all of these books.

If you would like to order any of the above titles please write to:

Age Exchange
The Reminiscence Centre
11 Blackheath Village
London SE3 9LA

or telephone 081-318 9105.

Reminiscence Boxes: Theme based boxes containing between fifteen and thirty objects, plus specially prepared ideas and guidance notes, sufficient for several sessions. An exciting new idea in which groups can see, feel and smell the past. Ten different themes currently available.

If readers are interested in hiring our touring exhibitions of photographs, or our reminiscence boxes, they should contact us at the above address.

The Age Exchange Reminiscence Centre in Blackheath, South-East London